ARTMAKER™



# Calligraphy

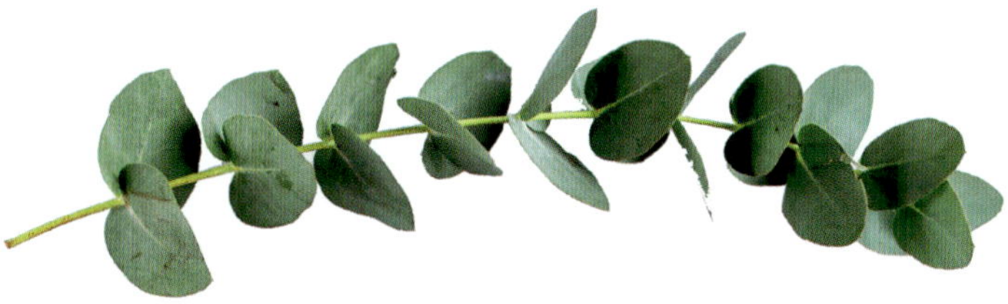

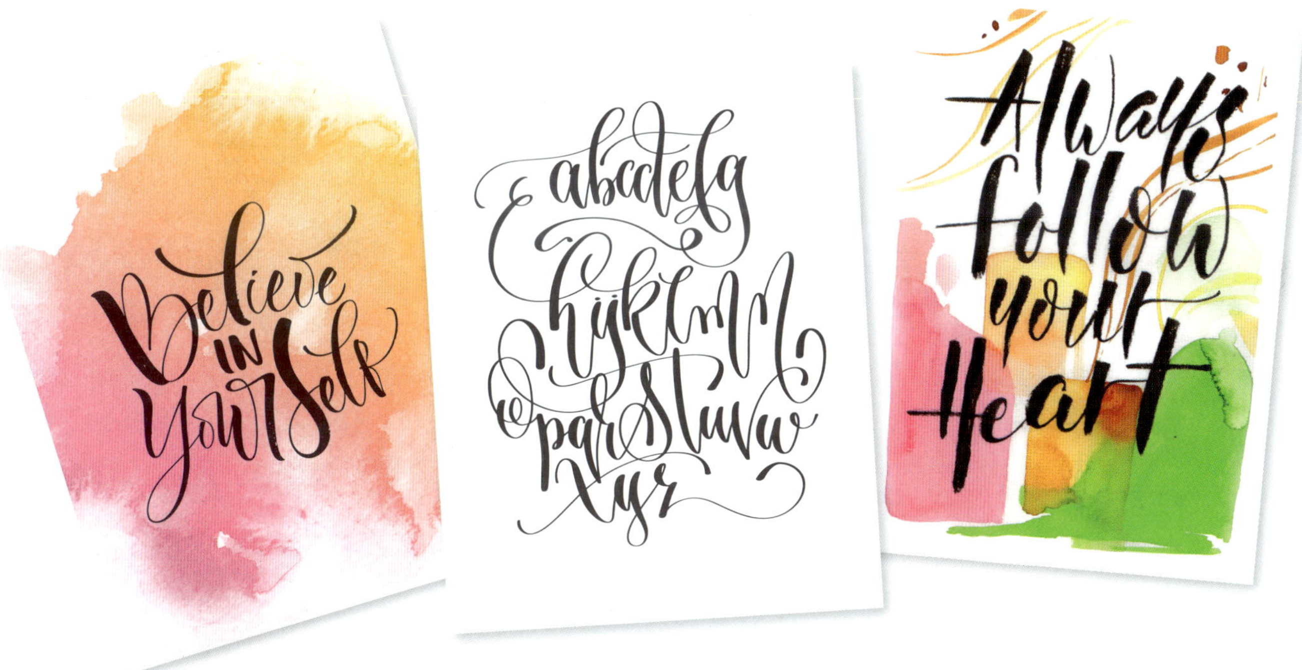


hinkler

# CONTENTS

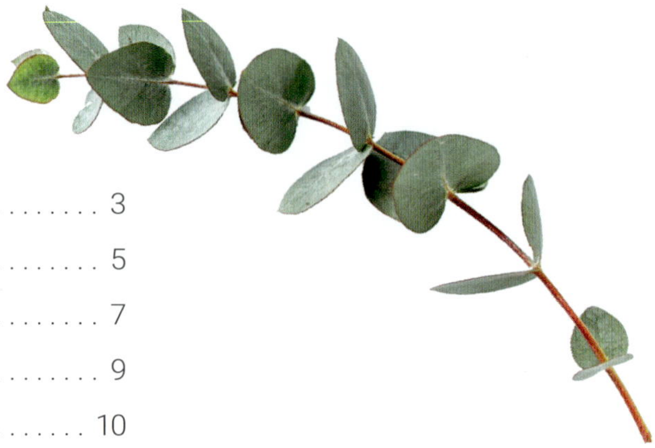



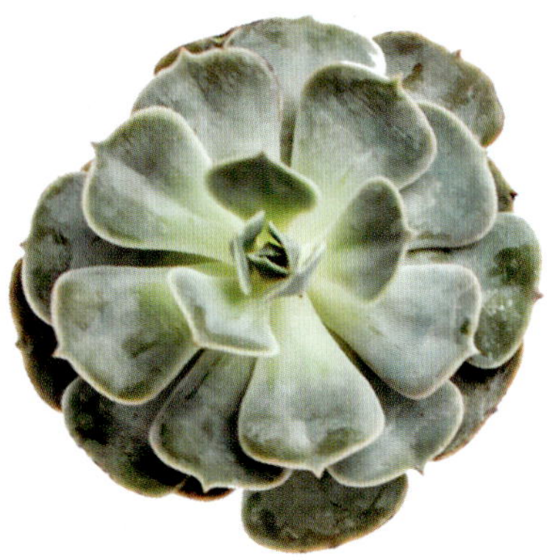


hinkler

Published by Hinkler Pty Ltd
45–55 Fairchild Street
Heatherton Victoria 3202 Australia
www.hinkler.com





Authors: Joanna Chia and Peter Taylor
Design: Lisa Howard and Hinkler Studio

Cover design: Hinkler Studio





ISBN: 978 1 4889 4926 5

Printed and bound in Ningbo, Zhejiang, China


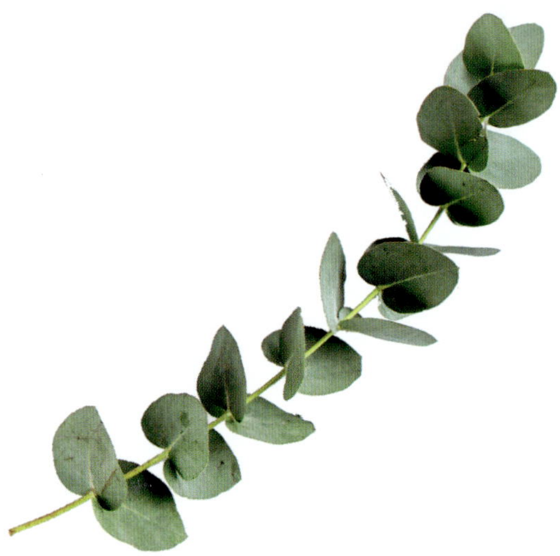

# INTRODUCTION TO CALLIGRAPHY

The dictionary says that calligraphy means 'beautiful handwriting', but these days, calligraphy is a lot more than that. Letters can be engraved into glass, carved into stone and wood, modelled in clay and created as pop-up sculptures. Calligraphy is seen on everything from advertising and product branding to greeting cards, wedding invitations and decorative artwork.

Back in the early days of handwritten books, all lines of writing were straight and evenly spaced. Over the last few years, instead of using letters and words traditionally, calligraphers have experimented with treating them like brush strokes in a picture; as little parts of an overall design. Lines of writing may now be uneven, curved or spiralled, or the letters jumbled to create particular special effects. Though most calligraphy is done with a square-ended, chisel-shaped pen nib that produces thick and thin letter strokes, from time to time today's calligraphers may choose to use any item that will produce a visible mark.

The aim of this book is to help you enjoy 'the artistic design and use of hand-created letters' while taking you through different techniques and calligraphy styles.

If you've heard the term 'modern calligraphy', you might be wondering exactly what it is! In a modern context, it might be easier to think of traditional calligraphy styles as an assortment of different fonts, where each 'font' originates from a different historical period and place.

Each traditional calligraphy style is characterised by its own unique features: for example, it may be written at a set angle or with very particular proportions and ratios. This way, every alphabet looks uniform and can be replicated over and over again.

In contrast to traditional calligraphy, which is a lot more rigid, has a lot more 'rules' and can look very formal, modern calligraphy is playful, expressive and a more relaxed take on its traditional roots.

**CALLIGRAPHY VS HANDWRITING**

The secret is out ... calligraphers can have messy handwriting! Calligraphy is carefully producing each letter as a drawing and placing it in the right spot. It's a totally separate skill from everyday handwriting, though some people do choose to base their handwriting on a calligraphy style.

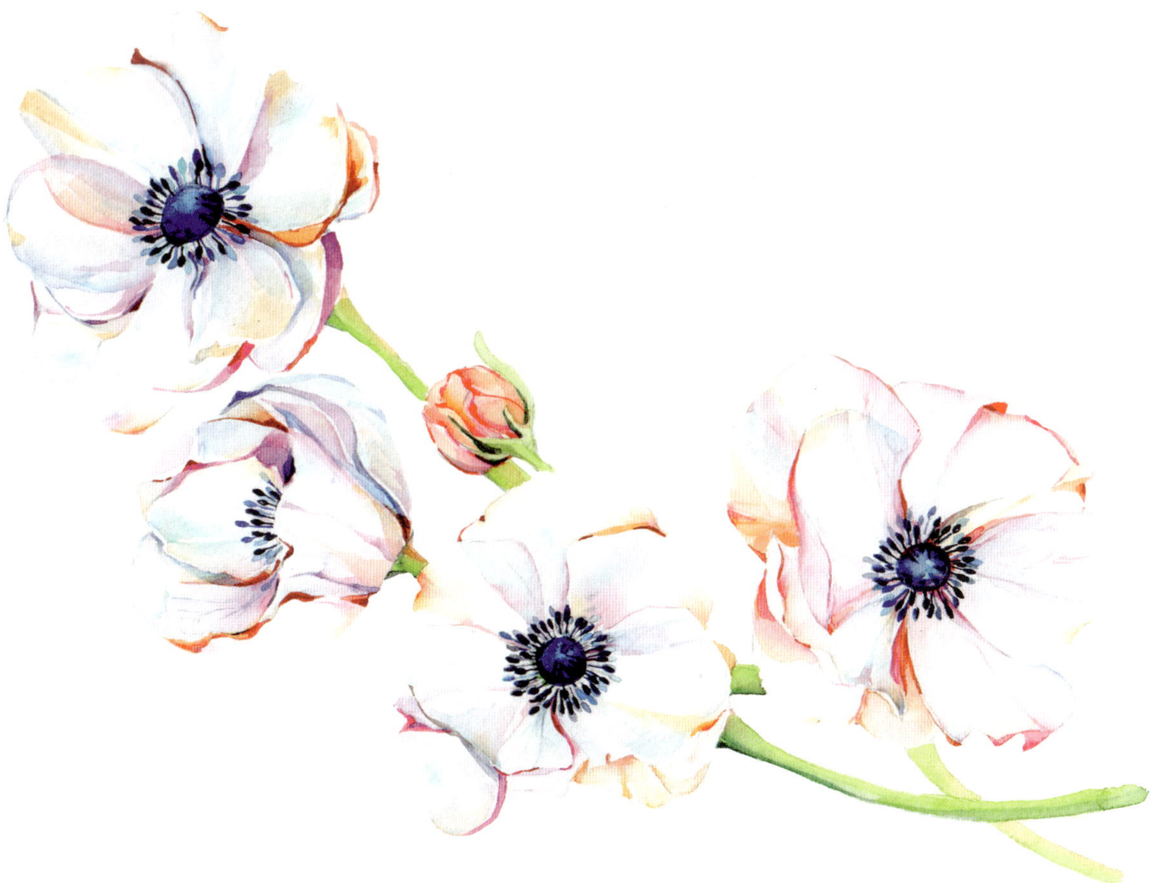

## LEARNING CALLIGRAPHY

This book will show you how to enjoy calligraphy – to write and draw letters and create finished work. It will also help you understand what to aim for when writing in particular styles.

It's a feature of being human that our hands don't always follow the instructions given by our brains. Even experts can find something in their finished piece of calligraphy that they wish they could change. Most artists feel the same about their paintings. But we have to aim for perfection. There is more chance of producing impressive writing and letter shapes if we understand the principles of their construction and how styles fit together. And like learning to play a musical instrument, the more you practise, the better you get and eventually you rarely need to think about the letter shapes and rhythms of different styles. When these come automatically, you can then concentrate on good spacing and working artistically . . . and you make fewer spelling mistakes (they're easily made when you're thinking of several things at the same time).

## DEVELOPING TECHNIQUE

To express yourself using calligraphy, you will want to collect a 'toolbox' of techniques and writing styles that you can select from and which you enjoy using. And by understanding the principles or rules of good letter construction, with practice, you'll become confident as a craftsperson, knowing what you are doing and why. People will recognise this confidence in your artwork – it's the hallmark of the finest calligraphy.

## PREPARING TO WRITE

### Position and posture

The best place to write is generally by a window on the shaded side of the house. If you're right-handed, have the light coming from the left and vice versa.

At night, try to sit so that a light provides illumination from a similar direction. An adjustable lamp should ensure you always have the light in the right place, but be careful as some may get too hot.

You have to be comfortable to write well, sitting with a straight back, square on to the board you'll use and the table supporting it, and with both feet on the floor.

### Writing board and surface

Some people buy hinged constructions for their writing board or prop it up on paper-covered bricks, but it works just as well to have the bottom edge in your lap and by moving closer or further away from the table, you can alter the board's slope.

The aim is for your forearm to rest completely on the board with your writing hand at least a third of the way down from the top. This keeps you steady and gives you better control.

Changing the slope of the board lets you control the speed at which the ink or paint flows from the pen – a shallow board angle makes you hold the pen more upright, and the ink flows quicker. It also gives you a better view of what you're doing.

If you put your paper straight on to the board, the surface may feel too hard. Calligraphy pens work best if the writing paper has a little bit of give or springiness under it. So, when you're ready to work on individual sheets of paper, it's a good idea to create a pad where you will write. Some calligraphers cover their whole board in sheets of newspaper and tape a large sheet of cartridge paper over the top.

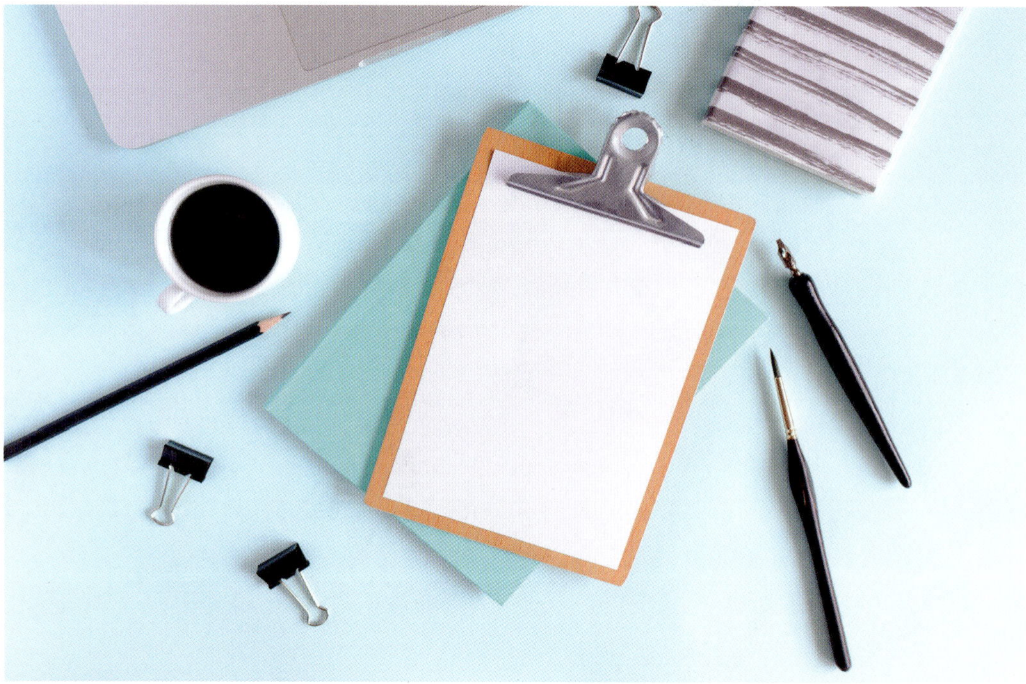

# WHAT YOU NEED TO GET STARTED

You don't need much to get started. In fact, you probably already have all that you need. It's a good idea to first draw letters with a single line – with a pencil, ballpoint pen, fine technical pen or fibre-tip pen. Any smooth paper they'll easily write on will be just fine. If you're keen to recycle and save the planet, you can write on the backs of used envelopes, around the borders of magazines or on advertising junk mail, but if you're buying paper for practice, the cheapest is probably photocopier or laser printer paper.

## CALLIGRAPHY PENS

**Calligraphy felt pens:** These pens usually have chisel-shaped tips that can rapidly wear out – sometimes after less than a page of practice. If you own one, keep it for an occasional letter or two when you have sharpened your skills.

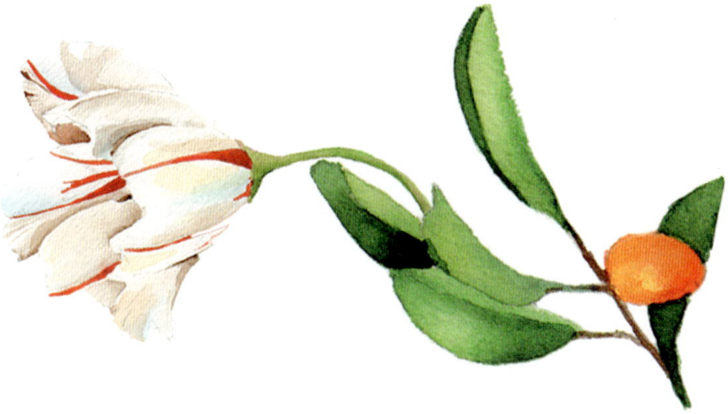

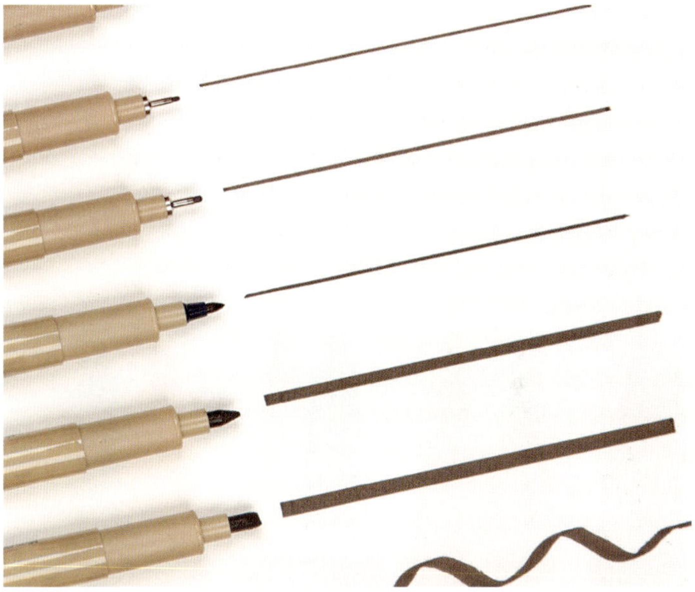

**Calligraphy fountain pens:** Many people will already own a calligraphy fountain pen or set of pens. They all work well. If you are going to buy this kind of pen, it's worth going to a specialist pen store to purchase one that you can refill from a bottle of ink, rather than having to keep using cartridges. Cartridge ink will eventually fade, but you can buy fade-proof ink in bottles.

If you are buying a pen with only one nib, choose a nib that's at least 1.9 mm (0.07 in) wide to learn with – the wider the better. Sets of pens usually come with a nib of this size, plus one smaller and one bigger.

If you get hooked on calligraphy, you will probably buy a complete pen for each nib size that you regularly use.

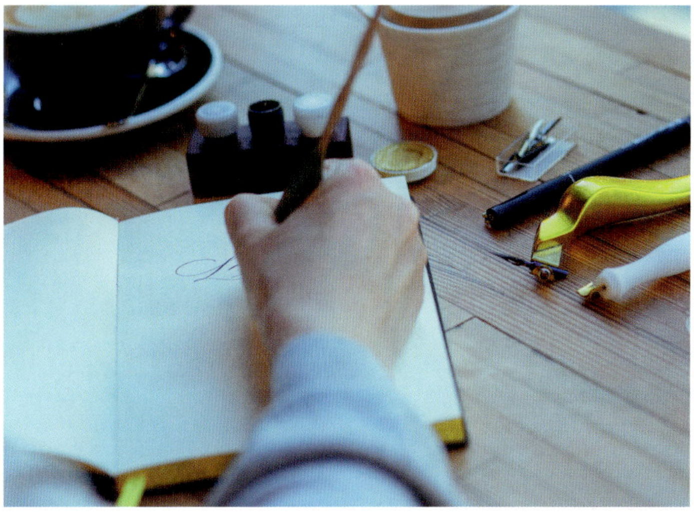

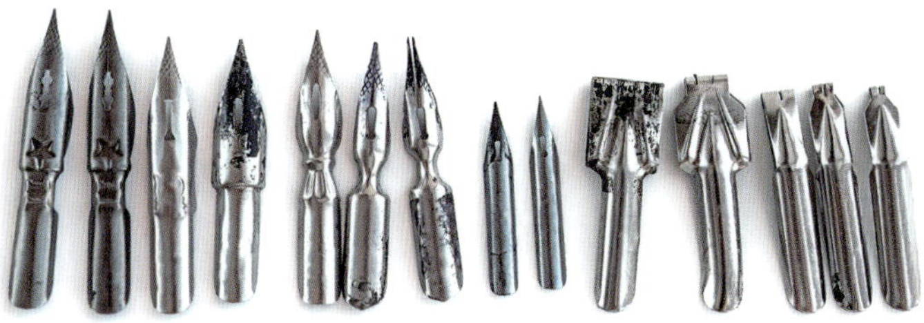

## BRUSH MARKERS OR BRUSH PENS

Brush markers, sometimes known as brush pens, have flexible brush tips to produce thick and thin line variations. They are usually filled with different coloured inks. Not only are they portable and easy to clean up, they also give you fantastic results when used properly.

There are many different manufacturers of brush pens. After a bit of exploring and experimenting, which brush pen you choose ultimately depends on a mix of personal preference as well as application. Generally though, these pens can be divided into a few different types:

**Felt tip brush pens:** These are stiffer than nylon and water brush pens, making them ideal for beginners who may not yet know how to control the pressure applied on the brushes. Unfortunately, this stiffness also means there is little contrast between thick and thin strokes. These are also usually single-coloured brush pens, which means you'll need several pens to get a gradient of different hues and colours.

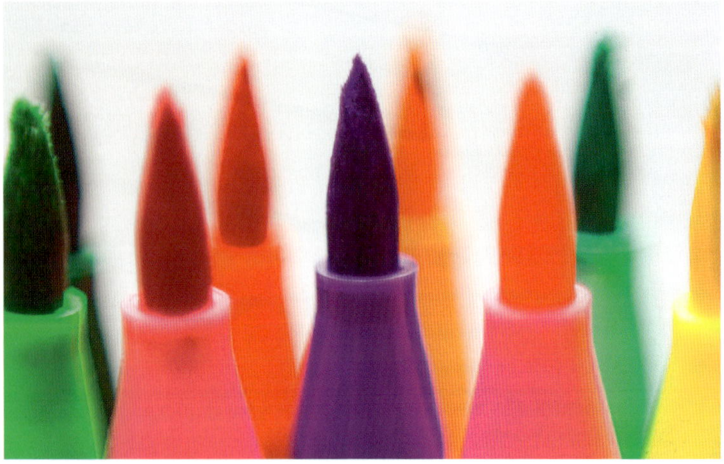

**Nylon brush pens:** Similar to felt tip brush pens, these pens are usually single-colour pens. The bristles, however, are much softer, resulting in a more flexible tip. This translates into a bigger contrast between the thick and thin strokes.

**Water brush pens:** These have a barrel in the handle that serves as a reservoir for water, and they are great for working with different liquid mediums. They benefit from the flexibility of nylon tips and the versatility of being able to create lettering with different colours without having to carry around many single-coloured brushes. Unfortunately, they can be hard to control because of the constant flow of water from the reservoir in the handle out through the tip.

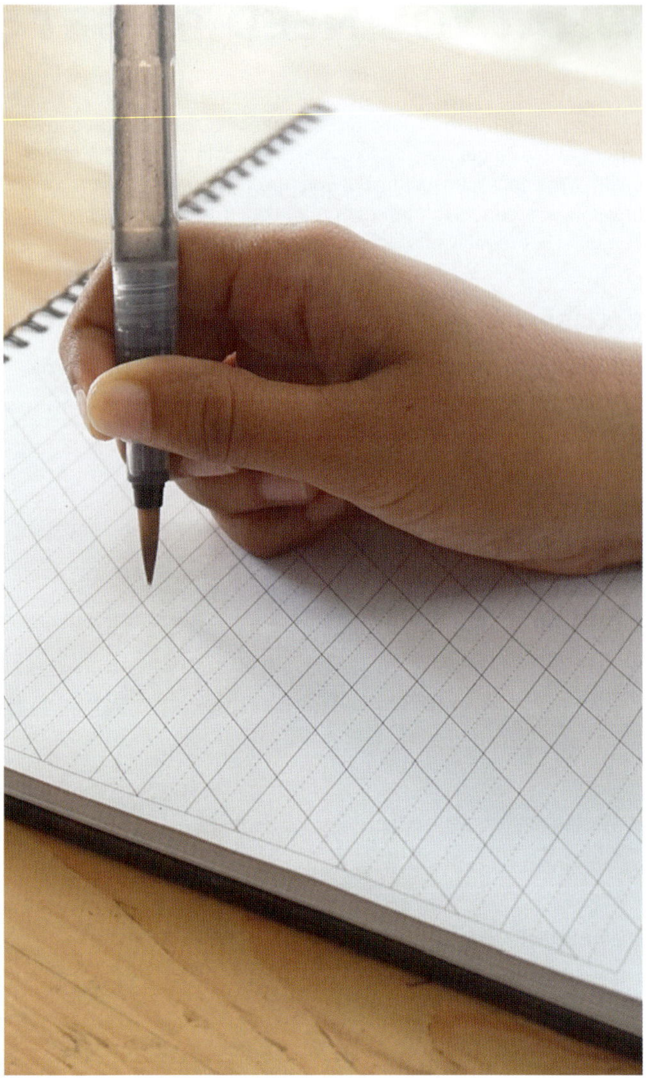

**RECOMMENDED KIT**

You will only need basic stationery items from around the house to get started:

- Ruler (preferably clear plastic)
- 2 HB pencils
- Sticky tape
- Scissors
- The side of a corrugated-cardboard box

# LETTER FORMATION

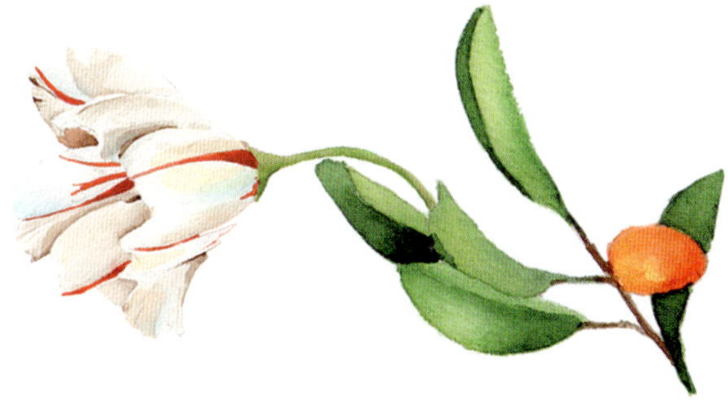

Now that you know a little more about what modern calligraphy is, it's time to learn how to use your tools to create beautiful lettering. In this section, you will learn about the anatomy or the components that make up a letter, how these letters are formed and how to piece them together to form words and sentences.

## ANATOMY OF A LETTER

Did you know that letters are actually made up of separate components or parts, and, just like humans, these can be broken down anatomically? Like the anatomy of a human body, these separate components serve specific functions, and naming them makes it easier for designers to communicate ideas. By changing the features of these separate components, you can alter the mood, style or 'voice' of the final lettering style. Figures 1a and 1b show the basic anatomy of type, which consists of:

- **Ascender loops:** the top part of tall letters such as 'h', 'l' and 'k' are known as ascenders
- **Bowl:** the curve that encloses a counter seen in letters such 'a', 'd' and 'o'.
- **Crossbars:** these refer to the horizontal strokes on letters like 't'.
- **Descender loops:** the descender refers to the bottom of a lowercase letter that extends below the baseline, as in the letters 'g', 'y' and 'j'. Some letters have a shorter descender, such as the letter 'p', although this line still extends below the baseline.
- **Entry and exit strokes:** these act as the links that join one letter to the next, i.e. the exit stroke of a preceding letter will function as the entry stroke of the next letter.
- **Flourishes/swashes:** often used as a decorative element, sometimes swashes or flourishes are used to fill up empty spaces in a layout, or to help a word look balanced when completed.
- **Serif:** is a small line attached to the end of a larger stroke, stem or crossbar of a letter.
- **Counter:** the empty space or hole of a letter that is either partially or fully enclosed.

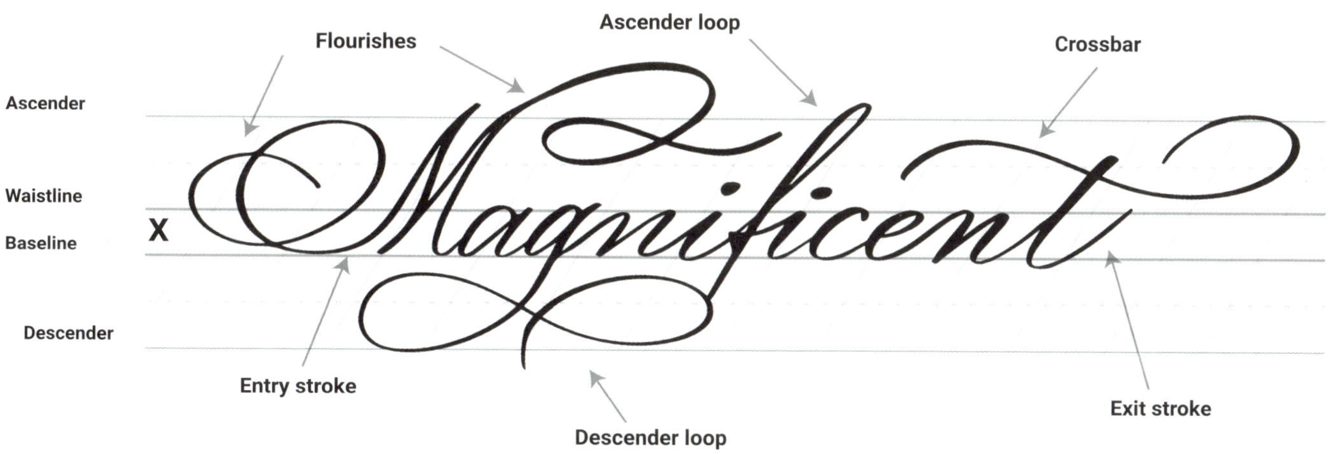


*Figure 1a: Anatomy of type*

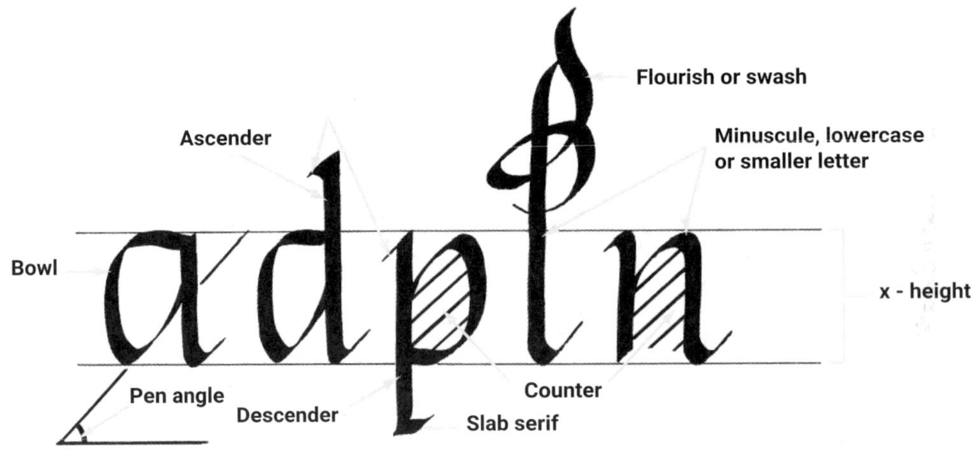


*Figure 1b: Anatomy of type*

## USING GUIDELINES

Do you want to know one of the secrets to great calligraphy? Using the right guidelines! When you're learning a new style, it is often helpful to follow along with the assistance of guidelines. These guidelines not only serve as a template for you to practise your letters on, they are also a practical way of ensuring you develop the right muscle memory moving forward.

You'll notice in Figure 2 that guidelines are made up of specific lines, such as the:

- **Ascender:** The first line from the top. This is where the tops of tall letters like 'l', 'k' and 'h' touch.
- **Waistline:** Where the top of short letters such as 'a', 'e', 'i', 'o' and 'u' touch. In other words, it measures the top height of these letters.
- **Baseline:** Where all your letters sit on a straight line. In modern calligraphy, the baseline acts as a relative guide, but it is still important to practise with it in mind when you're starting out.
- **Descender:** The lowest line. It functions as the boundary where the descenders or bottom parts of letters like 'y', 'g' and 'j' touch.
- **X-height/minim:** The height between the waistline and baseline. This is perhaps one of the most important measurements in brush calligraphy, as the other lines (ascender and descender) are measured relative to this height. If it makes it easier for you to remember, this is also the height of short letters such as 'a', 'e', 'i', 'o', 'u' and of course 'x' in a particular style.

*Figure 2: Example of guidelines*

# CHANGING LINE WEIGHTS

Here, we explore how to vary your line weights. This variation between the thick strokes (also known as shades) and the thin strokes (also known as hairlines) is what creates elegant and interesting contrasts.

## SHADES AND HAIRLINES

With the right techniques and tools, the variations in thick and thin strokes are achieved in a single clean movement. In calligraphy, these contrasting strokes are a result of varying the pressure applied while writing. In general, thick shades (usually written as downstrokes) are achieved by applying pressure on the tip, whereas thin hairlines (usually written as upstrokes) are achieved by relieving the pressure on your tip. If you're just starting out, it is useful to practise varying the pressure on your pen by repeatedly practising the basic strokes.

## BASIC STROKES

Throughout this book, you will find that letters are made up of combinations of a few standard basic strokes. Although there may be a few oddball combinations sprinkled around the letters of the alphabet, in general, the basic strokes form the bulk of calligraphy alphabets.

The task of breaking down alphabets into separate components isn't as daunting as it looks, as long as you focus on practising individual strokes separately. Developing a firm grasp of this concept will help you master the basic principles of calligraphy.

In these examples, follow along the directional arrows, which will guide you through the proper method of writing calligraphy scripts.

**Underturn**

Applying pressure on the tip of your pen, start with a downstroke that moves from left to right. Curve the stroke upwards to the right to end in a delicate upstroke.

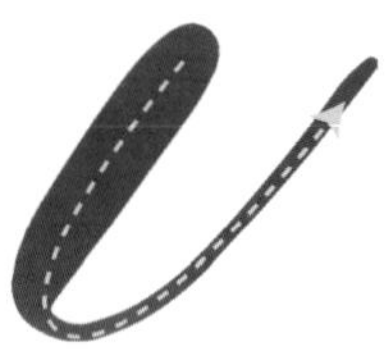

*Figure 3: Underturn stroke*

**Overturn**

This curves over from left to right, starting with a light upstroke and ending in a thicker downstroke. This is made by applying pressure on your pen as you do the downstroke.

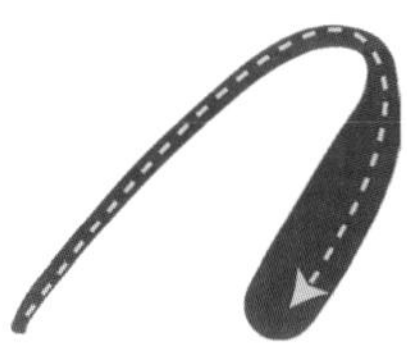

*Figure 4: Overturn stroke*

**Compound stroke**

Start as if you're drawing an overturn, but instead of stopping at the downstroke, curve upwards in a thin upstroke, as though you're joining an underturn to your previous stroke.

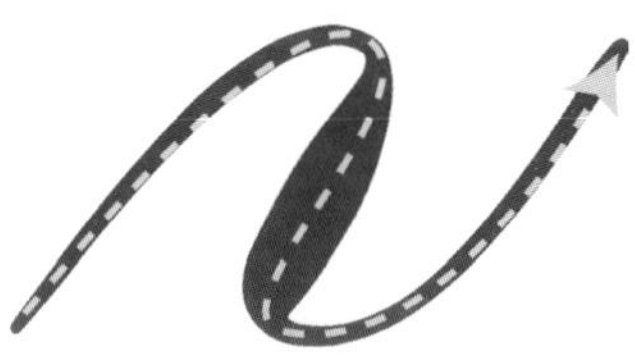

*Figure 5: Compound stroke*

**Ascender**

The ascender is the first stroke in letters like 'b', 'k' and 'l' and starts with a thin upstroke.

It curves into a thick downstroke, crossing over to the left of your initial upstroke.

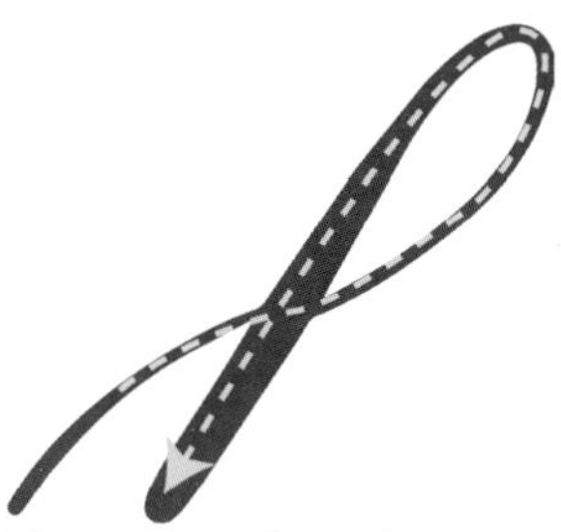

*Figure 6: Ascender stroke*

**Descender**

This extends below the baseline, and you'll see it in letters such as 'g', 'j' and 'y'. Start with a thick downstroke before curving over from the left to end in a delicate upstroke.

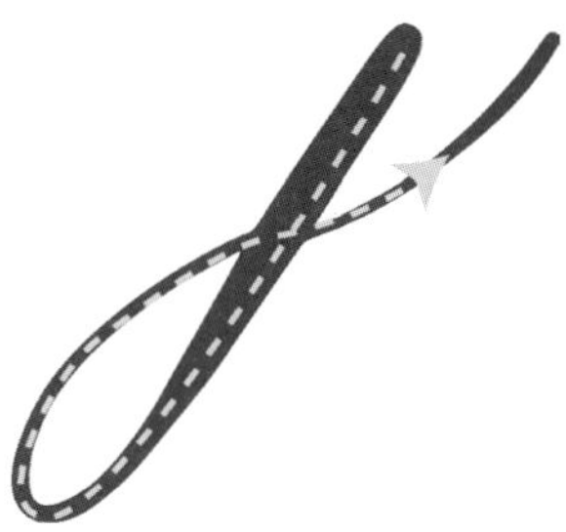

*Figure 7: Descender stroke*

**Ovals**

Imagine the face of a clock. Starting at '1 o'clock' and moving anti-clockwise, draw a thicker downstroke before curving upwards to complete the oval. Aim for elliptical or egg-shaped forms.

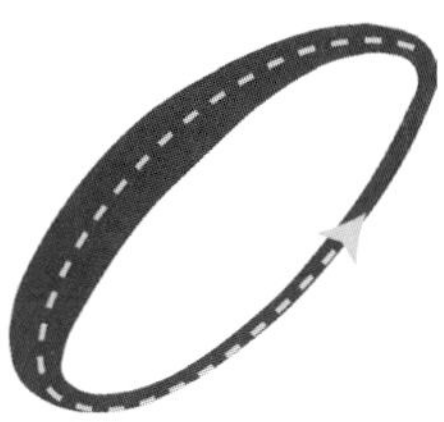

*Figure 8: Oval stroke*

# DIFFERENT STYLES OF CALLIGRAPHY

Different calligraphy styles can be combined and used together when composing your final artwork. Before we venture into more modern styles of calligraphy, it would be beneficial for you to understand how to break down traditional calligraphic alphabets into their separate components, as this will help you control the shapes and proportions of your letters.

In this section, you'll learn basic letterforms and how to connect them into words and eventually into full compositions. Although this may seem simple, it is important to master these concepts, as they lay down the foundation for more intricate styles.

## BASIC CALLIGRAPHY

This style is still very functional because it's very legible and is great for more formal, structured work. You can definitely use this for formal invitations or if you're trying to communicate ideas in a more serious manner.

### Lowercase letters

Remember when we learned about the basic strokes? In this section, you will study how these strokes interact to create the letterforms and alphabets we've come to know and love. Here you'll notice that almost all the letters of the lowercase alphabet are made up of a combination of basic strokes. Observe how the letters 'g' and 'a' are written.

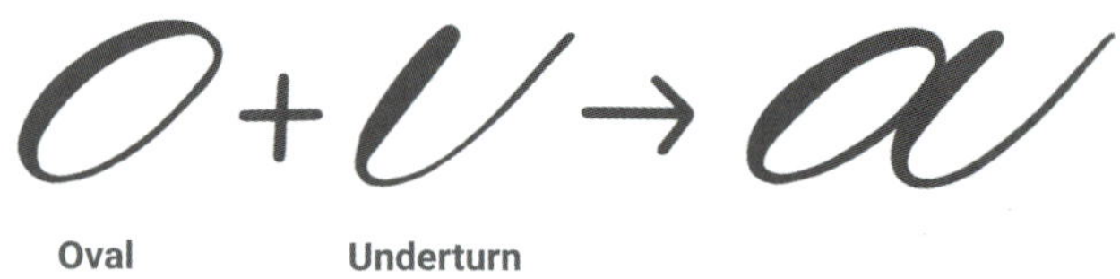


***Figure 9a: The letter 'a' is made up of a combination of an oval and an underturn.***

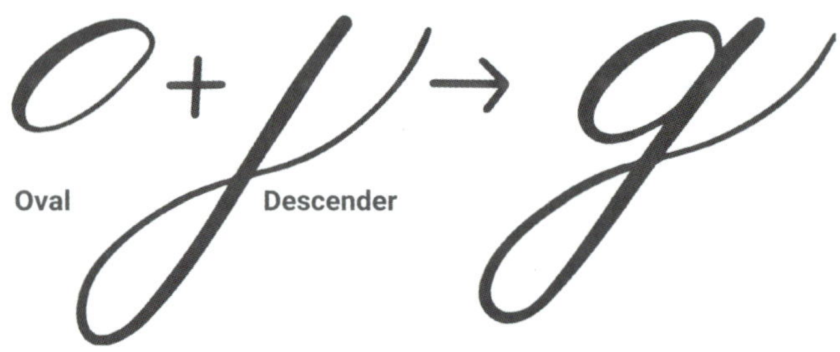


***Figure 9b: The letter 'g' is written by laying down an oval and descender as separate strokes and combining them together.***

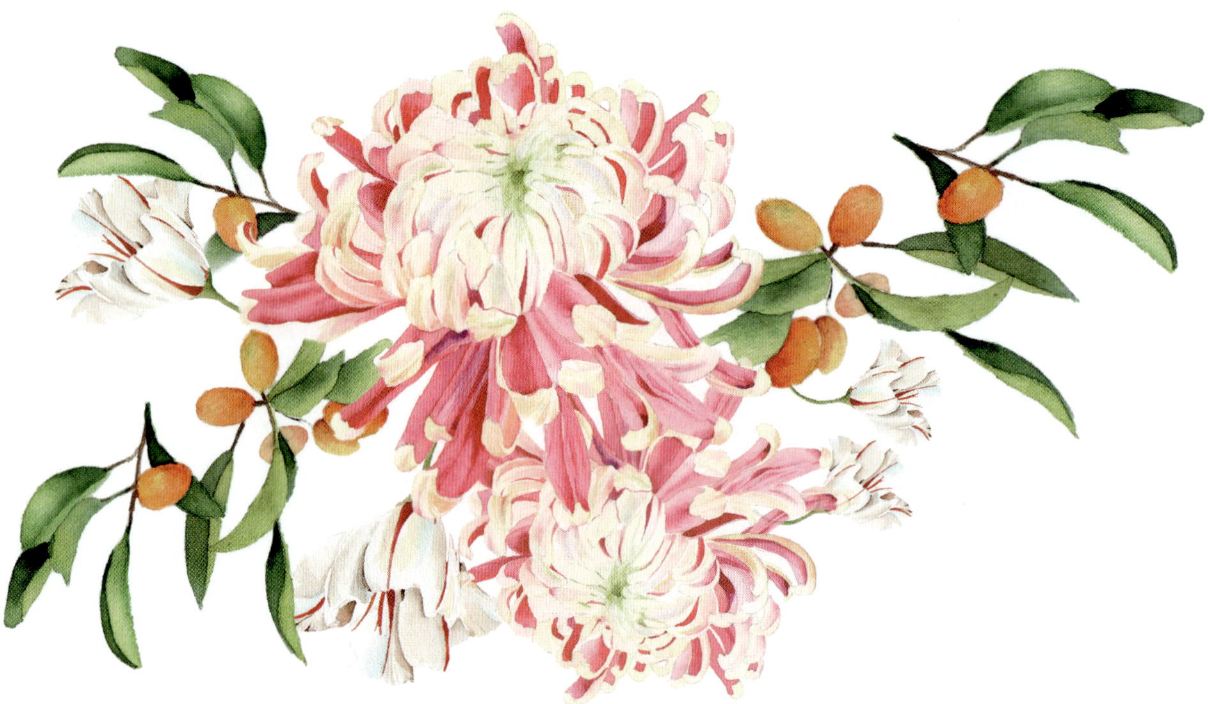

This piecing together of separate elements applies to all alphabet letters. Try to follow along the directional arrows on each letter, paying close attention and looking for the basic strokes of which each letter is composed.

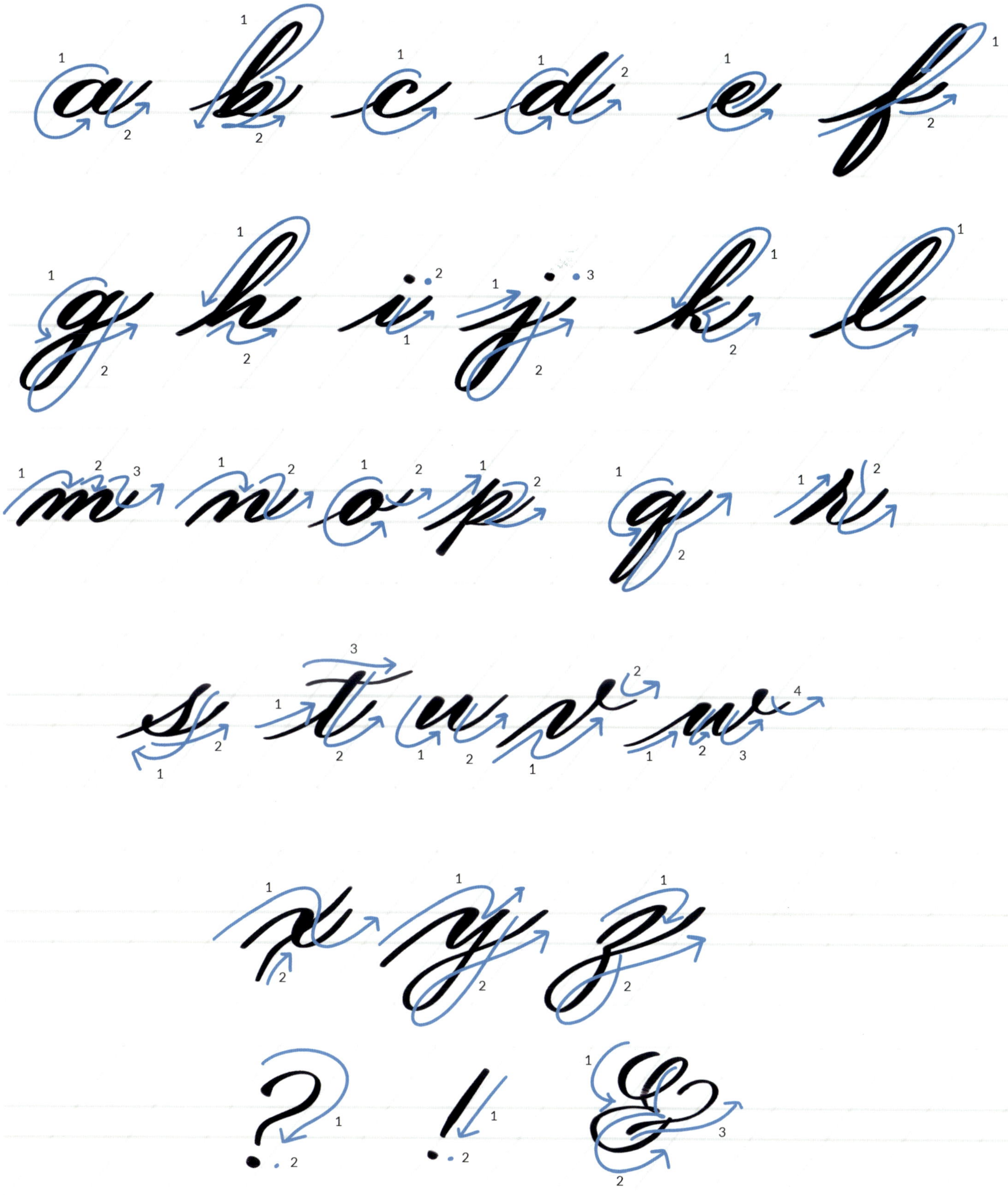

*Figure 10: Basic Calligraphy lowercase letters*

### Uppercase letters

Although it may not be as obvious as with the lowercase letters, the uppercase letters are also made up of repetitive basic strokes. As a rule of thumb, these letters are written from left to right, top to bottom. If you find yourself getting confused, there are numerical arrows along the examples to guide you. As always, remember that the shades are often written as downstrokes while the thinner hairlines are often done as upstrokes.

Similar to the lowercase letters, the uppercase letters can be broken down into individual strokes, as shown in the directional arrows indicated on the examples. Uppercase letters often have a capital stem, which functions as the reference point for the other strokes. This can be seen as the first stroke in letters like 'B', 'P', 'R' and more. Can you identify these strokes in the example shown below?

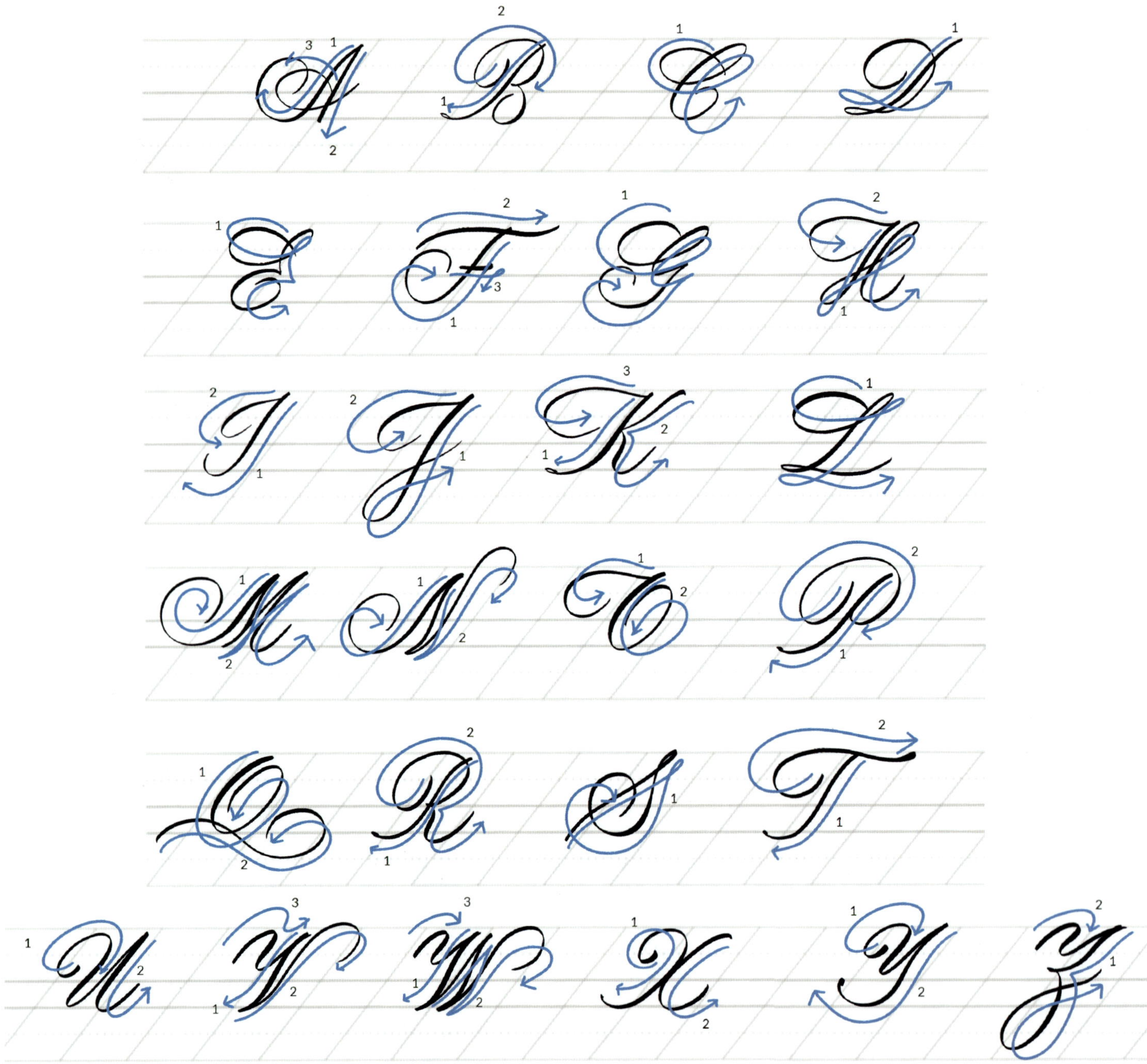

***Figure 11: Basic Calligraphy uppercase letters***

### Forming words

Now that it's time to write actual words, as beginners, you may be confused or tempted to write each word as a whole without lifting your brush. However, calligraphy is different from cursive writing, where writers 'join' letters together in order to write faster, while legibility and aesthetics are secondary. In contrast to this, calligraphy involves breaking down each word into individual letters, and then further breaking down these letters into the separate strokes that they are composed of. Although this may sound like a lot of thinking, with diligent practice, this will eventually become instinctive.

In Figure 12, the simple word 'holiday' can be broken down into separate strokes. The main benefit of doing this is that it allows you to maintain control over your letterforms, simply by controlling how each stroke looks.

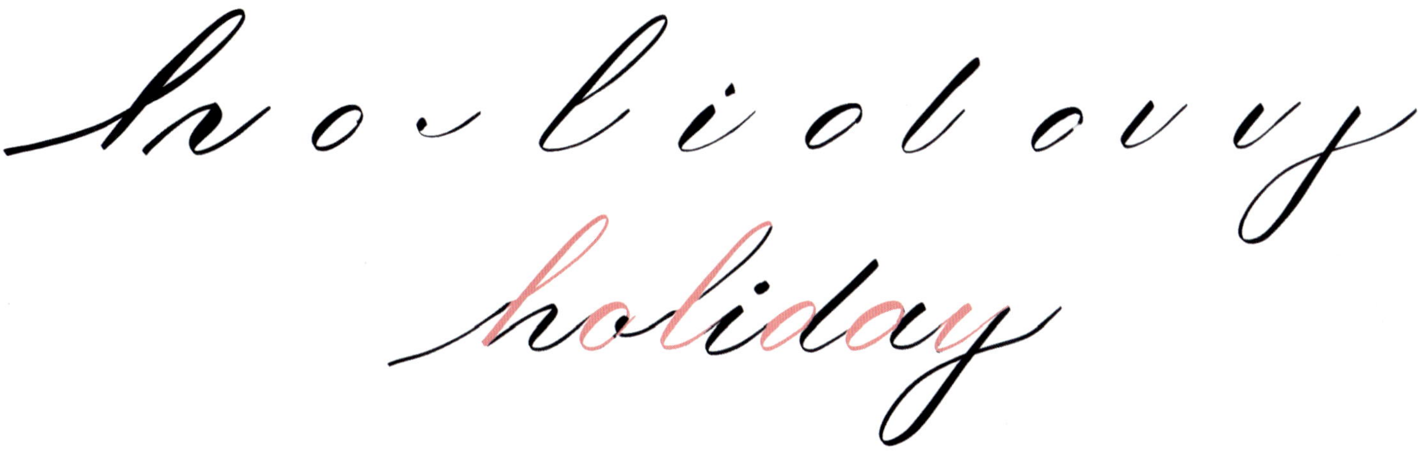


***Figure 12: Breaking down a word into the basic strokes of which it is composed***

### Connecting letters

Sometimes you'll come across letter combinations that are challenging to connect to another. An example of this is connecting the letter 'a' to the letter 'n'. As you can see in Figure 13a, the 'a' ends in an underturn, whereas an 'n' starts with an overturn stroke.

The way we connect this is by introducing a new stroke, which looks like a mirror image of the compound stroke. In Figure 13a, imagine that the width of one stroke is denoted by the width of a basic stroke (such as an overturn, underturn, ascender or descender). Notice how this new connecting stroke occupies the space of 1.5 times the width of a basic stroke.

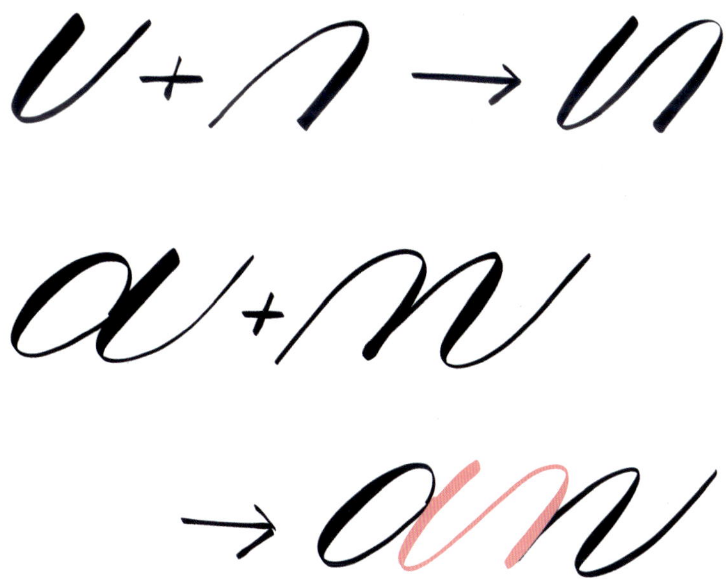

***Figure 13a: Letter connections, and the need to introduce new connecting strokes***

Another example of a non-conventional letter connection is when you need to connect letters that end with an underturn to a letter that starts with this stroke, which we'll call the filled-in dot. A practical example of this is when you need to connect the letter 'o' to the letter 'n'.

Figure 13b shows how we introduce the addition of another stroke, which also occupies the space of 1.5 times the width of a basic stroke.

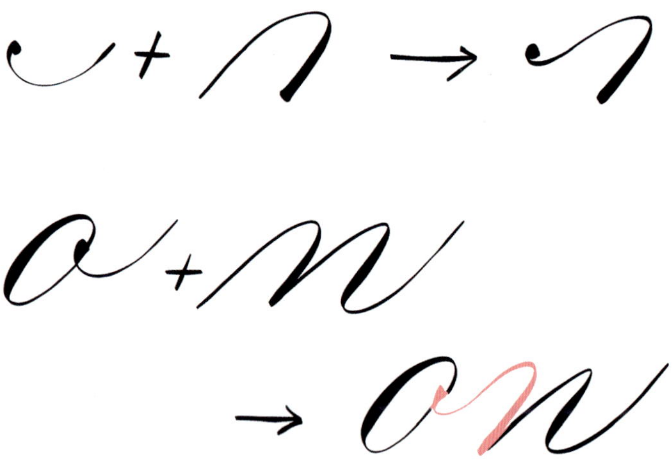

***Figure 13b: Letter connection between 'o' and 'n'***

Now that you've learned the basic strokes, proper letter proportions, and how to piece together separate strokes to form letters, it's time to put your new knowledge into practice. This is where the fun begins, so get out a piece of paper and practise forming words and composing layouts of your favourite quotes.

At the start, if you run out of ways to practise, look for pangrams, which are sentences that contain every letter of the alphabet. Some of these are rather quirky and provide hours of fun learning! You can also practise by writing out the lyrics to your favourite songs.

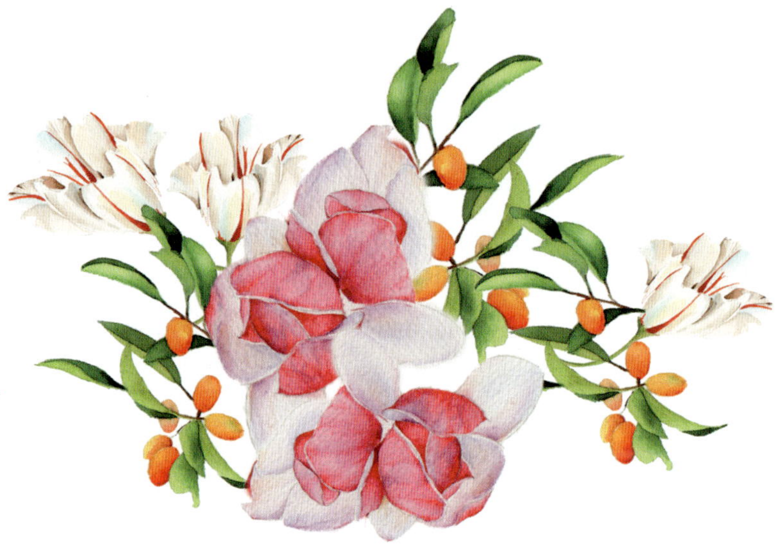

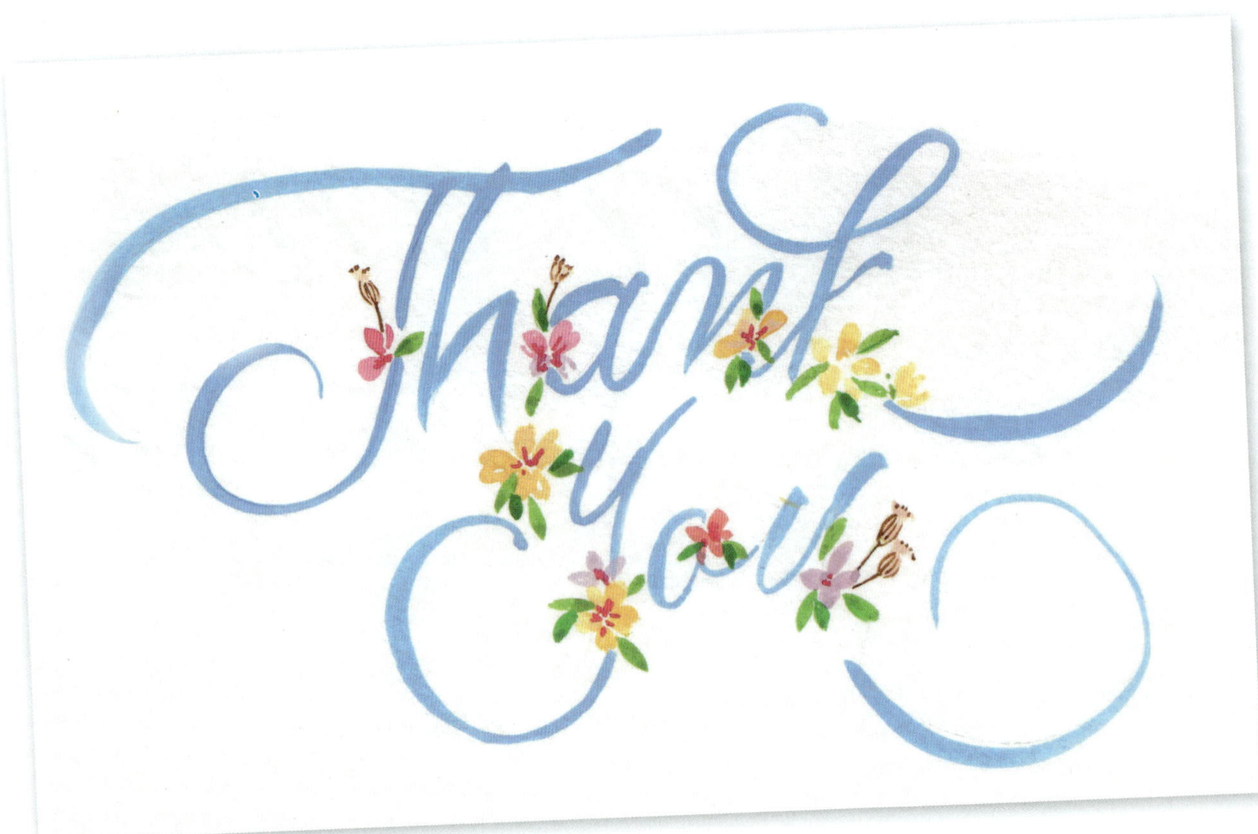

## FOUNDATIONAL HAND

Foundational Hand was first devised by Edward Johnston after studying the 10th-century book Ramsey Psalter, written in a Carolingian style.

It's upright, based on circles and has many features of elegant Roman letters and can also be easily modified to create interesting and useful variations.

As with learning Roman capitals, it's best to first learn the letter shapes and proportions by drawing simple versions with a pencil and fitting them into squares, as shown in Figure 14. Square-gridded paper is ideal to use to start with. Once you have mastered this, you can then begin to write the letters freehand on plain paper with top and bottom guidelines.

### Letter spacing

Next, try spacing out letters to write words. The space between letters should always appear to equal the same area as the white space counter inside the letter 'u', or 'n'.

Unfortunately, you can't rely on writing in boxes to space letters – it has to be done by eye. This can get tricky when an 'r' is followed by a 'v' for example. In that case, the top of the 'r' can be shortened, and the left corner of 'v' started fractionally lower than normal and tucked underneath. Similarly, the bar of 't' can be shortened when necessary, as shown in Figure 17.

The space between words should be about the complete width of the letter 'o', as shown in Figure 17. If an 'o' touched on to the right-hand end of one word, the following word would be touching the other side of the 'o'.

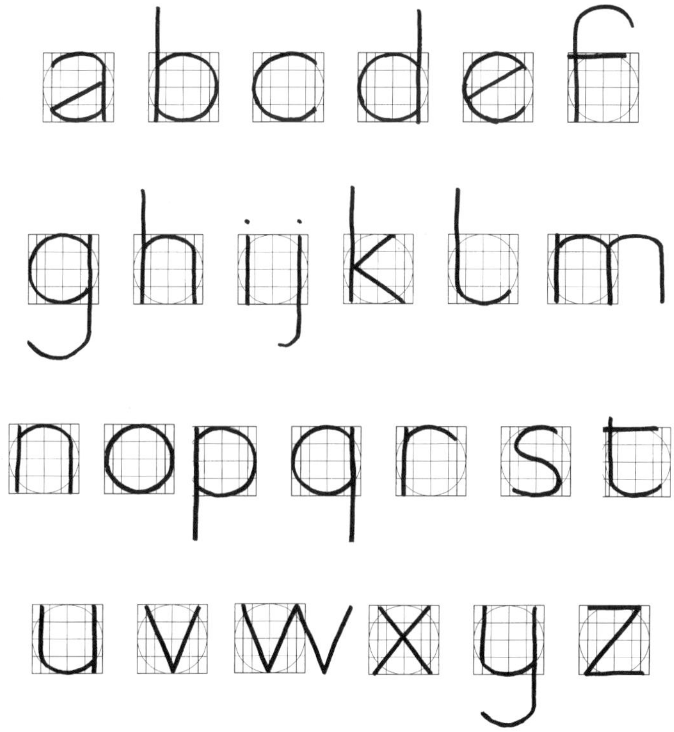


**Figure 14: Foundational Hand lowercase letters**

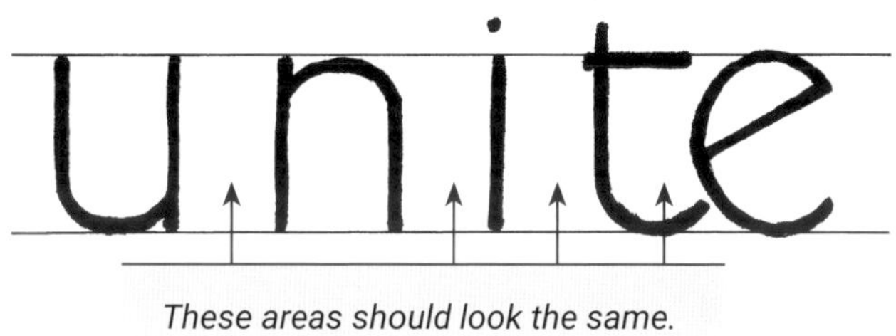


**Figure 15: Evenly spaced letters**

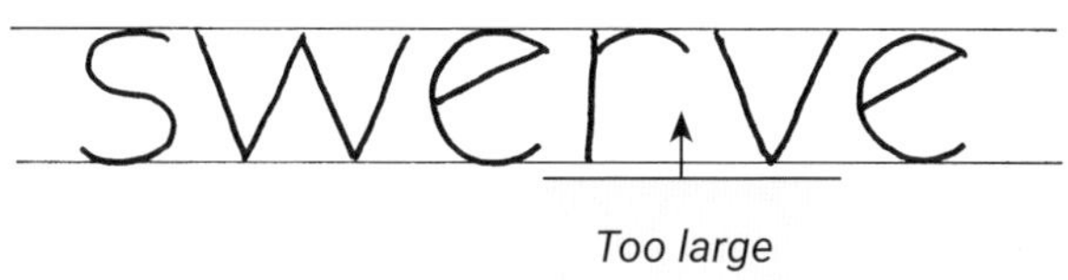


**Figure 16: An example of when there's a large space between letters**

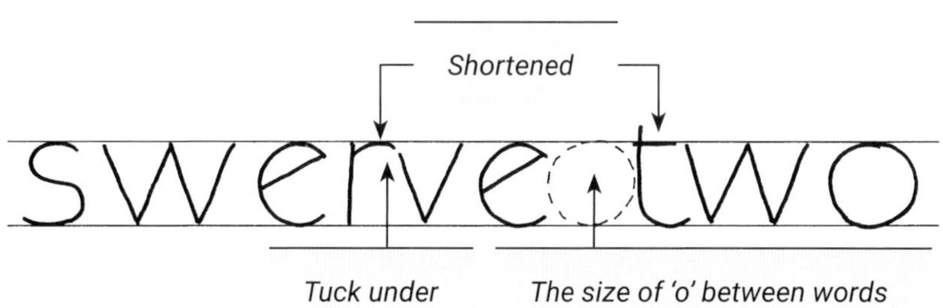


**Figure 17: Shortening the strokes of letters and spacing between words**

### Drawing the letters with nibs

Now, take out your calligraphy pen and let's try drawing the Foundational Hand letters with that!

By drawing with your pen, you will discover how to move and wiggle the nib from side to side to make straight lines that continue at hair thickness (as thin as the nib will make).

For Foundational Hand, you need to hold the pen and the paper so that these thin lines are about 35° to the horizontal. This is the pen angle. If you could remove your writing hand from the pen, the pen-handle would drop to land as in the picture to the right.

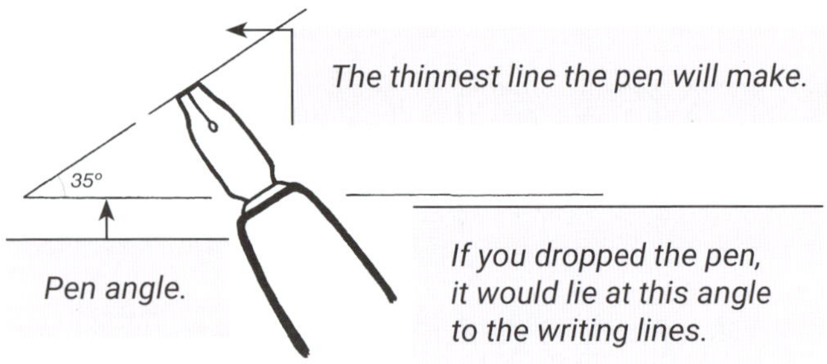


**Figure 18: Foundational Hand pen angle**

Your paper does not have to be vertical. If it helps you to maintain the correct pen angle, turn the paper a little, especially if you're left-handed. No matter what part of a letter you draw, your pen always stays at that 35° angle in this style.

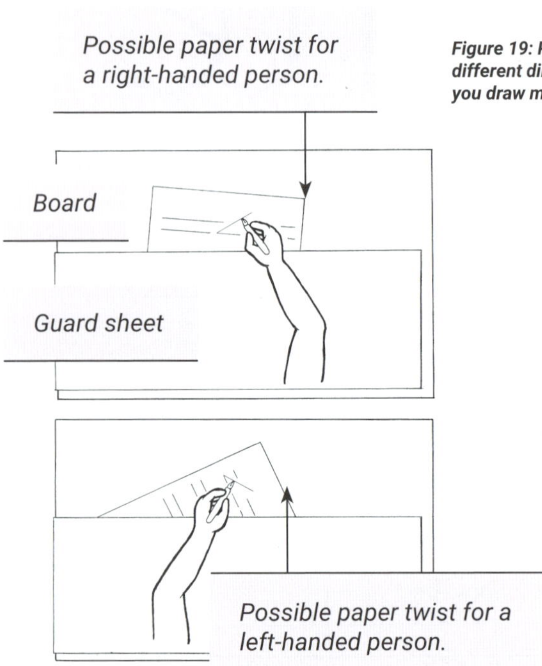


**Figure 19: Paper angled in different directions may help you draw more precise letters**

If you draw a vertical and a horizontal, the horizontal will be the thinner of the two.

Now, try to draw the same small letter shapes that you drew with a pencil. Remember, you are drawing letters, not writing. You will need to take your pen off the paper and construct many letters in a number of separate strokes.

Although the aim is to write between the guidelines, it's more important to make sure the letter shapes are correct. Take it above or below the lines if it creates a better shape.

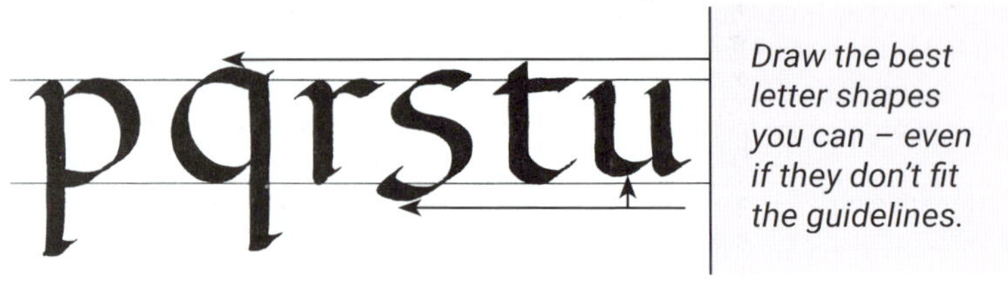


**Figure 20: Letters which have been drawn inside and outside the guidelines**

Dip nibs do not like being pushed on the paper. They are likely to dig in and the ink could splatter. Try to get into the habit of always pulling or sliding the pen whether you are using a dip pen, fountain pen or any other implement. It also means you can add attractive 'micro-commas' on the tips of the top element of letters like 'c', 's' and capital 'G', for example.

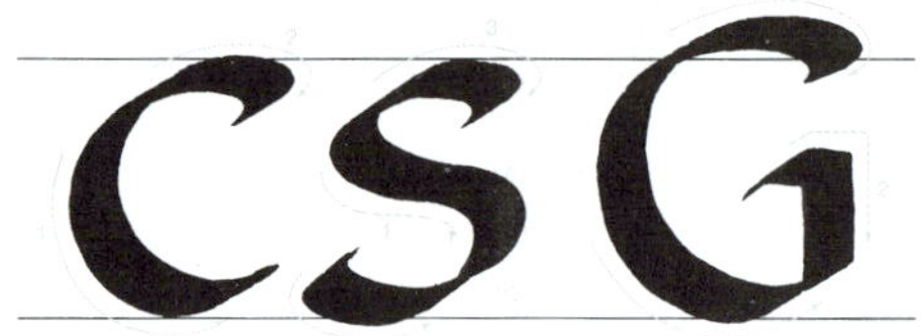


**Figure 21: Micro-commas on letters**

**HANDY TIP**

Your writing hand should stay in the same small area of your board. Your other hand moves the paper after every two or three letters. This helps you to maintain the correct pen angle at all times.

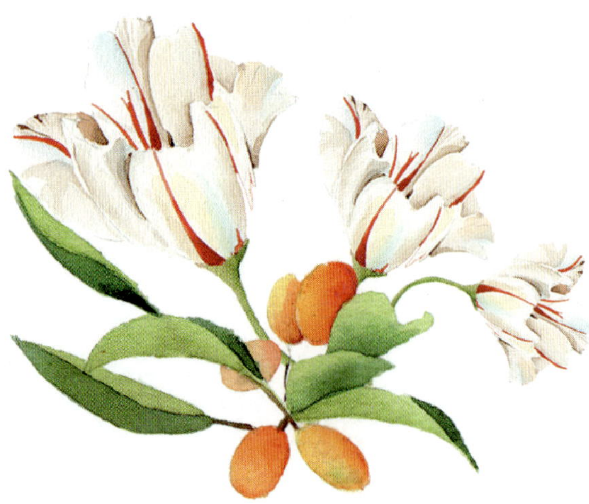

For an 'o', the centre of the pen follows two halves of a circle – left and right, starting close to the top line.

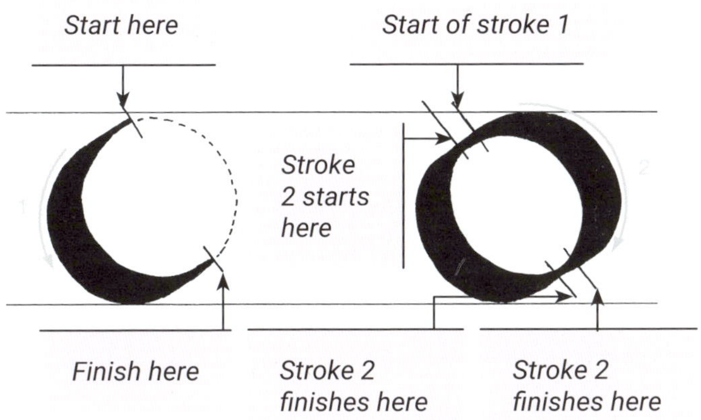


**Figure 22a: Drawing an 'o'**

When writing 'n', put the pen nib inside the vertical and start it moving around the arc as you construct the top curve. There should be no thin line showing. The same goes for other letters with rounded tops, and the reverse applies for 'u'.

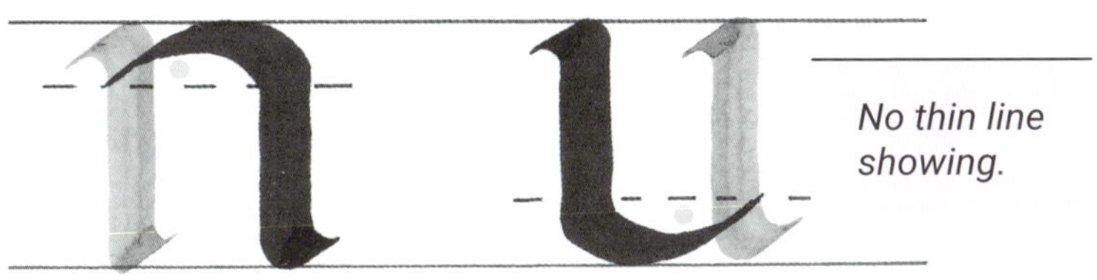


**Figure 22b: Drawing an 'n' and 'u'**

When you can easily draw these shapes, you can add some extra finishing strokes.

**HANDY TIP**

If you are ruling your own guidelines for Foundational Hand, rule the ascender and descender lines about 4 nib-widths above and below the main lines for the x-height.

Foundational Hand is based on a circular 'o' and so most added serif parts relate to circles. The top serif 'hook' should start curving straight away with no thin line sticking out, while the bottom 'hook' should similarly follow a circle and finish at a point without the thin line showing.

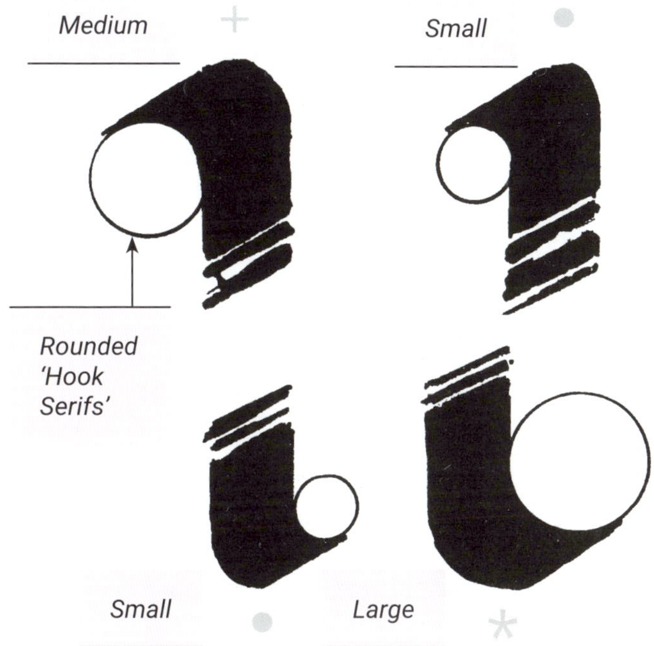


**Figure 23: Top and bottom, large and small serif hooks**

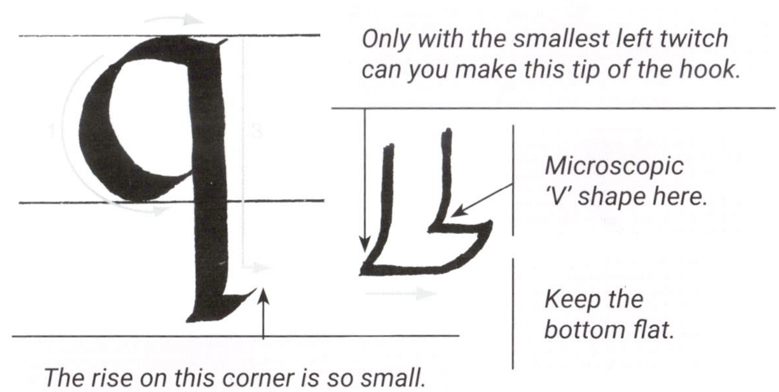


**Figure 24: Serif hooks on the letter 'q'**

On letters 'u', 'n', 'm' and 'h', the outside hook can be the same size or larger than the ones on the inside limbs.

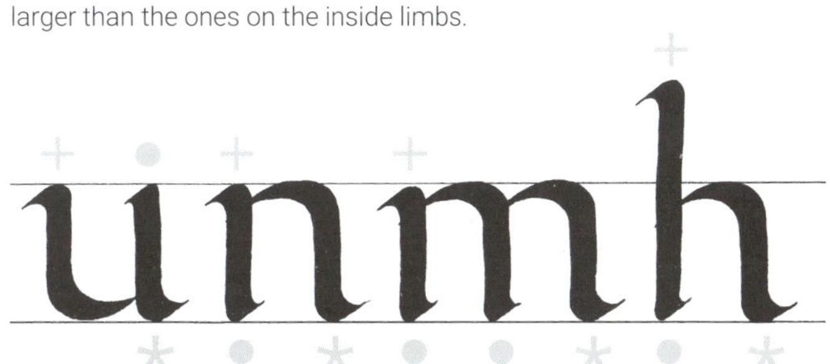


**Figure 25: Serif hooks on lowercase letters**

### Lowercase and uppercase letters

Below is the complete alphabet. This alphabet is straightforward, but not easy. Now you have all the alphabet, you can practise all the letters, numbers, symbols and any phrases. Remember to take your time!

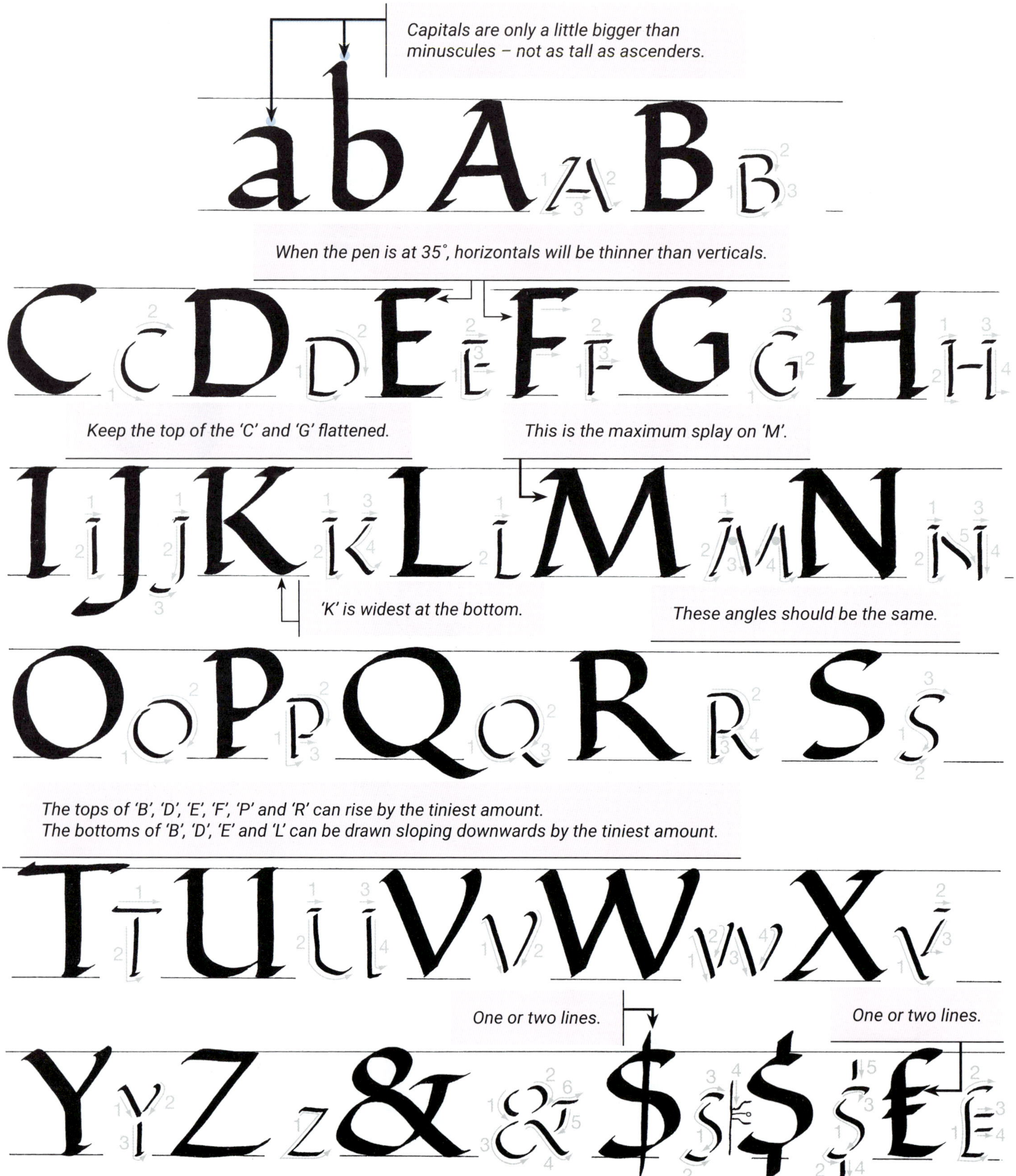


*Figure 26: Foundational Hand lowercase and uppercase letters*

## ITALIC

Over the centuries, Italic script has changed a lot and today calligraphers are still finding new ways to modify letters but retain the underlying principles of construction. Italic dates back to Niccolo Niccoli's bouncy joined handwriting of 1416. Later scribes cut off some of the joining strokes and added extra precision in the drawing of each letter for impressive documents, including copies of the Pope's instructions to be sent to all branches of the Roman Catholic Church in the late 1400s and early 1500s. When wealthy people saw the style, they paid for books to be written out with even greater care and no joins at all between letters. This became known as Formal Italic.

In the mid- to late-1500s, printing was taking over from writing, so scribes such as Arrighi, Cataneo and Tagliente earned money from teaching people how to write. They created rules for proper letter construction and had copybooks printed, but it wasn't long before the skills of the original scribes were lost.

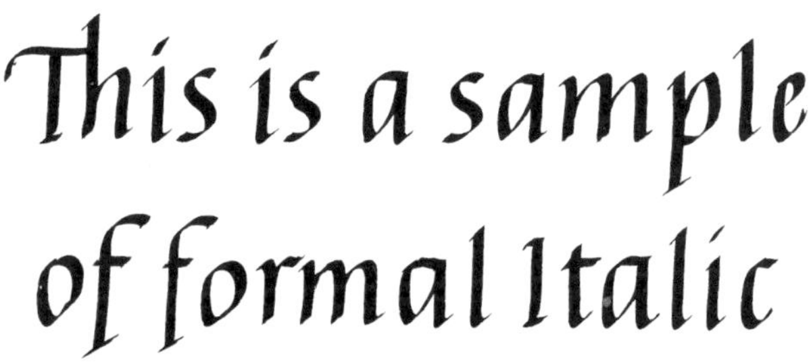


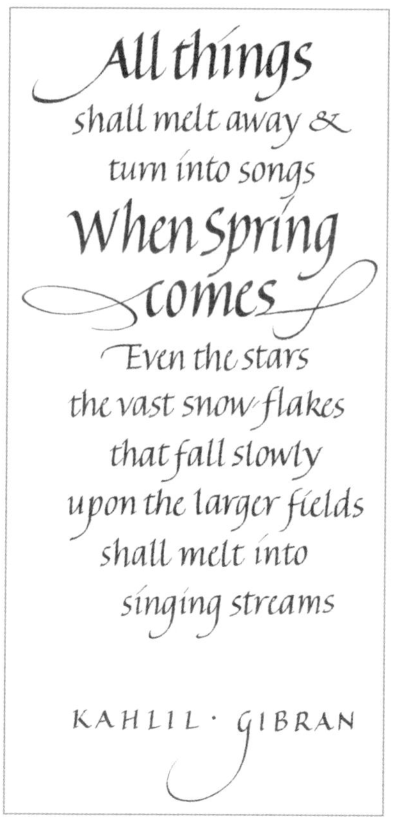


***Figure 27: 'All Things', by Kahlil Gibran, calligraphy by Gaynor Goffe, a left-handed calligrapher. This artwork is from the collection of Barbara Nichol, The Pen Shoppe, Brisbane. It has been written in Italic.***

Italic handwriting became popular during the 20th century, particularly after 1932, when Alfred Fairbank designed modernised letters (based on Arrighi's) for student use.

Early Italic writing was incredibly small and it was easy for a worn quill pen to be pushed around the writing surface, but you can't easily push modern metal dip nibs.

Italic calligraphy using large-sized letters has only been popular since the mid-1900s. It shares many features with Italic handwriting, but is not just a larger version. As with Foundational and Gothic styles, many of the calligraphic Italic letters are constructed in several separate strokes.

The characteristics of Italic are that the letter 'o' is compressed – it's elliptical – and the arch shape on 'n' branches out from the vertical.

The Italic writing style is often called the script of 'branching arches'. Like all other alphabets, it is controlled by the shape of the letter 'O'. Because it is narrow, so are all the other letters. When written with 'bounce', it is usually also slightly sloped, because slope comes naturally as speed is increased. To start with, and also for important documents like certificate designs, it's best to keep letters nearly upright. The branch feature comes when drawing an 'n' and related letters. Having reached the bottom of the vertical, the writing implement stays on the paper, backtracks a tiny distance back up the vertical and then branches out and heads in a smooth arc towards the top right hand corner of the letter, where a sharp but rounded turn is made before descending parallel to the first stroke.

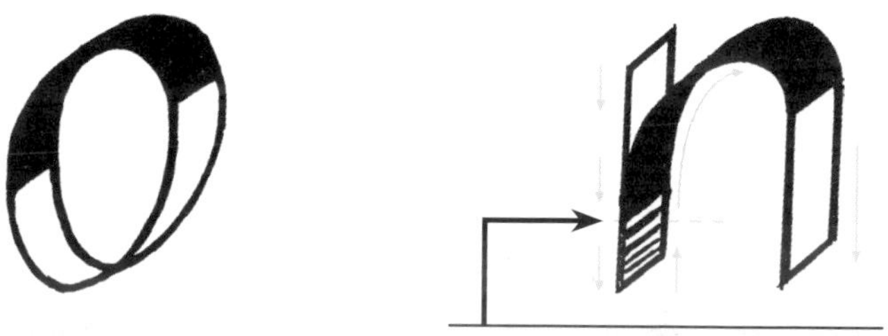

*The shape and slope of 'o' controls those features of other letters.*

*'n' branches from this level after the pen nib has backtracked up the vertical.*

***Figure 28: Italic 'o' and 'n' characteristics***

Try the alphabet first as skeleton letters as shown below. The top right-hand corner of 'u' and related letters is the reverse of the bottom left-hand corner of 'n' – the sloping line of 'u' is pushed vertically as it finishes, and this tip is covered over as the right-hand side descends. Then write the letters with tiny entry and exit strokes. Pointed 'tick' entries can be added to the tops of 'i', 'l', 'v', 'u', 'w', 'y', 'j', 'h', 'b', 'p' and 'k'. The exit strokes are rounded and, if extended, would be lines drawn at about 45°. The reverse is used for the rounded entry strokes to 'n', 'm', 'r' and 'x'.

Capitals are best kept simple and with classic proportions, though perhaps with all of them squashed a little from side to side, too.

Note how a capital 'A' will fit into the wedge shapes created on branching Italic letters. Also note the relationship between 'b' and 'g'.

When writing thick and thin calligraphy for any given lettering style, 99 per cent of the time, the pen should be held at a constant angle to the writing line – for an upright Italic this is about 45° (it can be good to increase the pen angle when writing the verticals on a letter 'N', for example). Remember, it's often easiest to maintain this 45° angle if you move the paper every few letters.

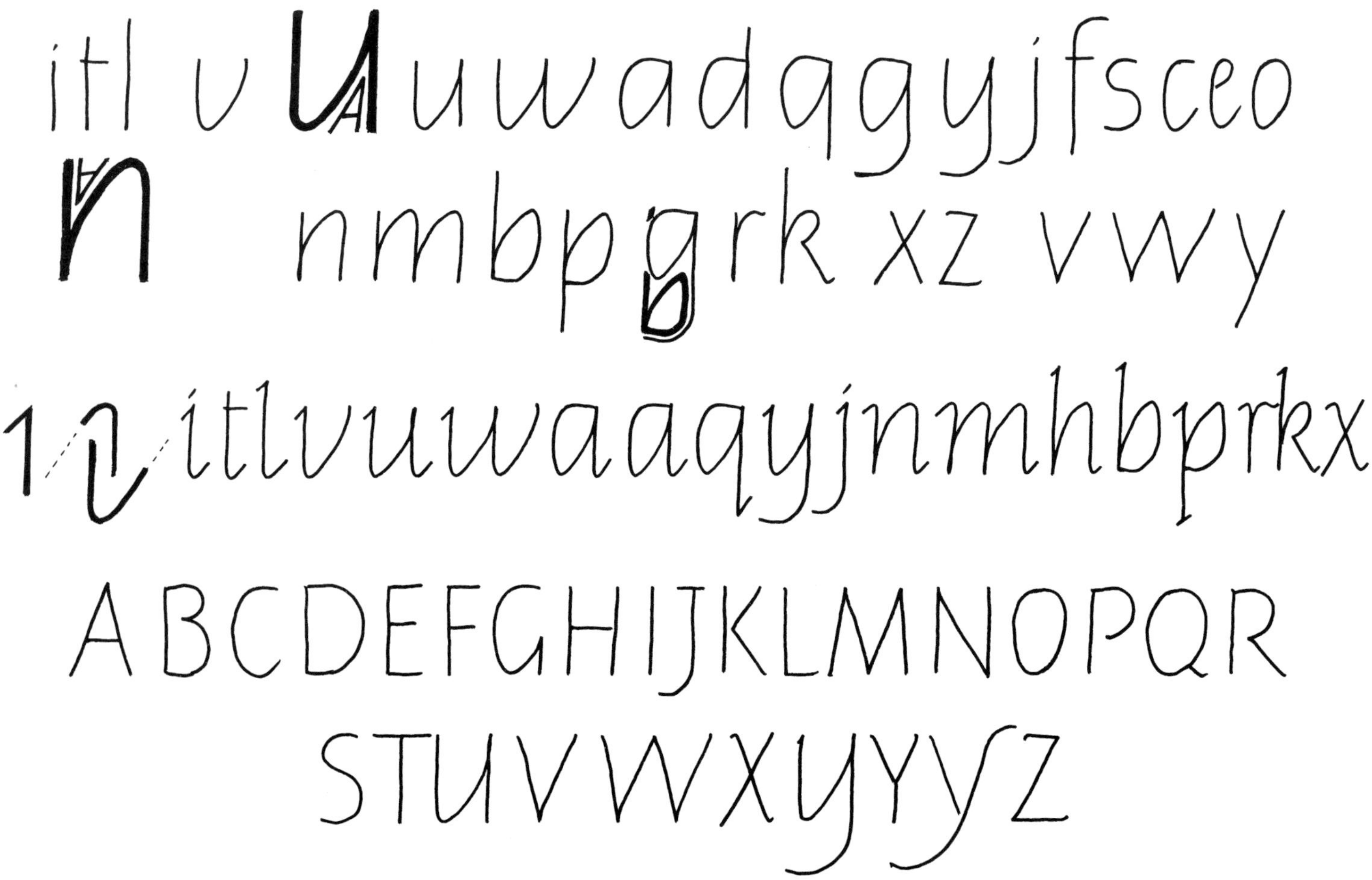


***Figure 29: Italic skeleton uppercase and lowercase letters***

### Lowercase letters and numbers

If you are ruling guidelines yourself, the usual x-height of Italic small letters (lowercase or minuscules) is five times the nib-width. This alphabet is built in families of letters. Use the below as a guide and then turn the page to practise these lowercase letters, their alternative versions, and their numbers.

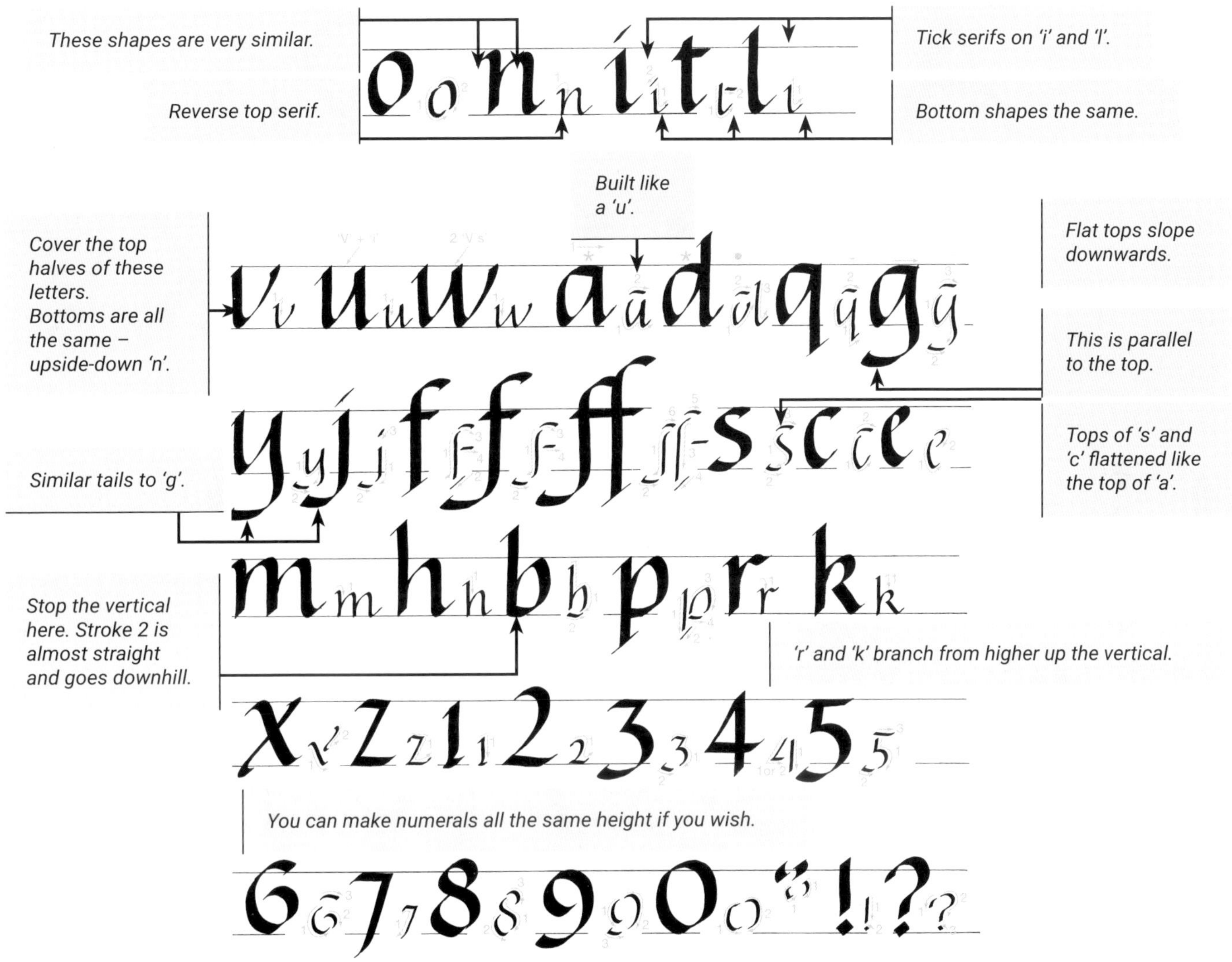


**Figure 30: Italic lowercase letters and numbers**

Some alternative letters are shown below.

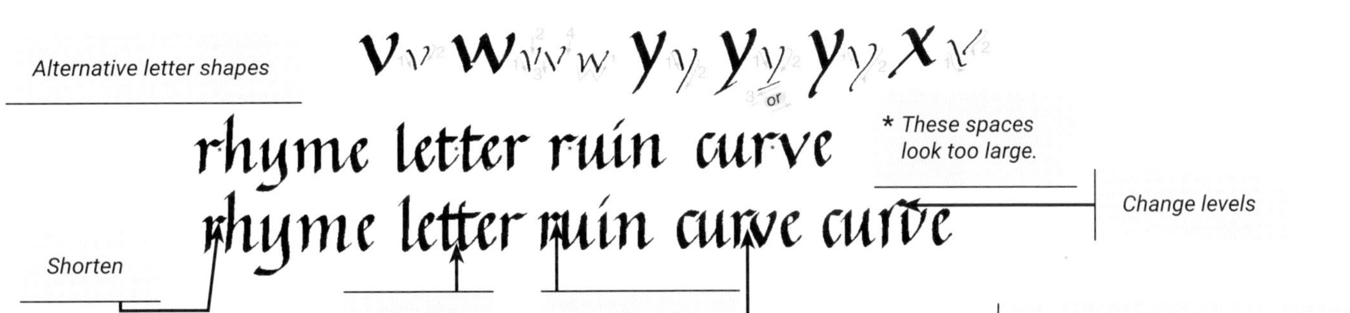


**Figure 31: Alternative Italic letters**

### Uppercase letters

Italic capitals are 6.5 nib-widths high. They can be less sloped and compressed than the small letters. Most capitals look best when drawn only a small amount taller than minuscules. Now that you have learned all the letters, you can practise your italics skills.

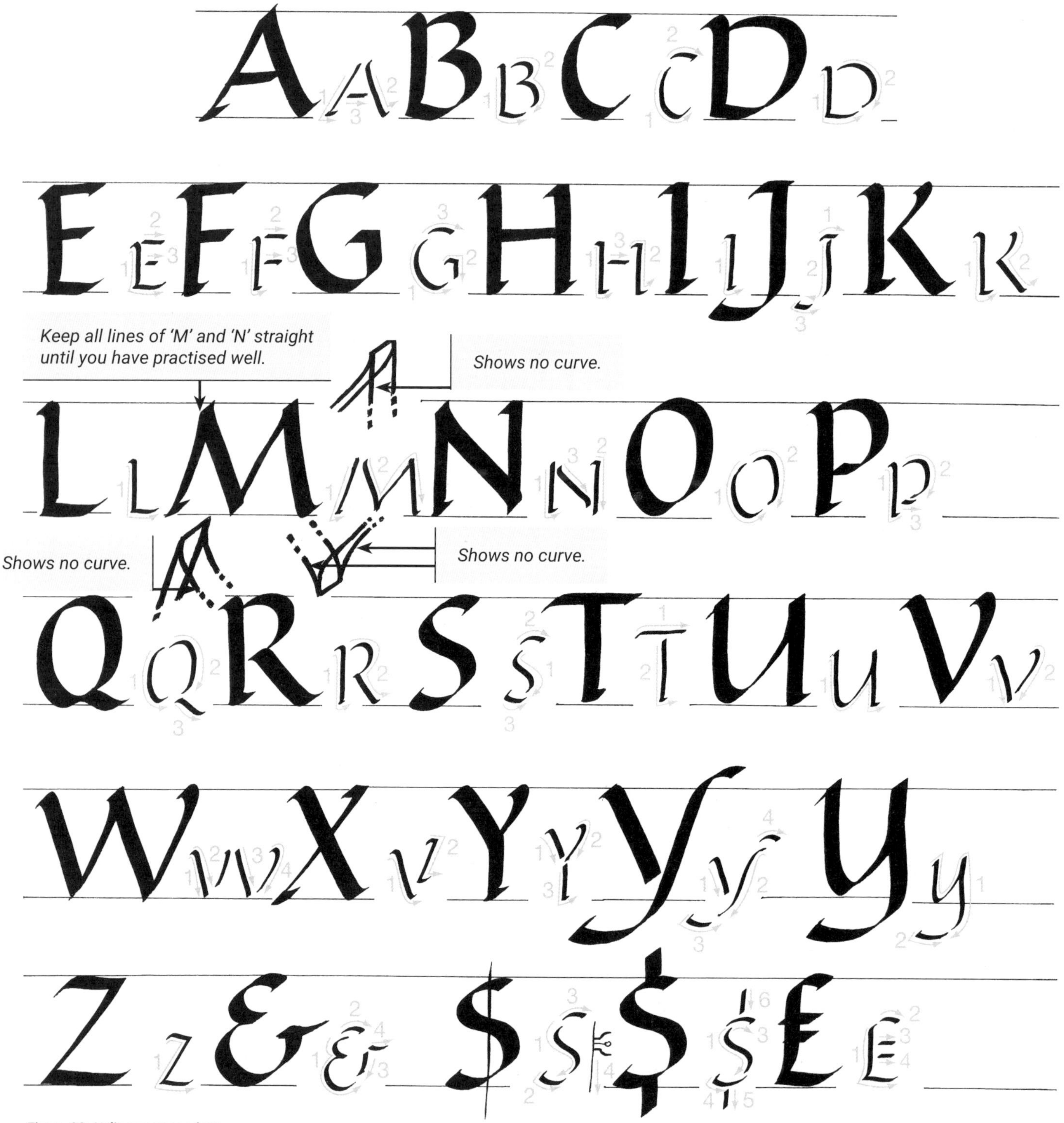


*Figure 32: Italic uppercase letters*

## MODERN BRUSH SCRIPT

A modern, expressive style, this script is great for adding a touch of sharp contrast in your letters through the drastic difference between the thick and thin strokes. Due to the versatility of this contemporary take on calligraphy, this style is fast becoming more popular owing to its increased legibility and less traditional look. It is also more minimalistic, meaning that it doesn't have as many flourishes when compared to other calligraphy styles, thus appealing to a younger, more modern audience.

Try this style on expressive works. Due to the sharp contrasts, and the way the swift brush strokes are captured, this style is particularly great for modern styled artworks.

### Lowercase letters

The lowercase letters in this style consist of modified versions of your basic strokes. For instance, instead of closing the loop of the oval that forms the first part of the lowercase 'a' in Basic Calligraphy style, you may leave it slightly open in order to capture the gesture of a stroke that was written with quick precision. The exit strokes in this style don't necessarily allow the letters to connect, unlike in other styles.

These strokes show a greater contrast between the thick and thin lines and do not flow seamlessly from stroke to stroke. This deliberate break in rhythm gives it an expressive, gestural feel, and the reader can almost feel the quick strokes of the brush which is a feature of modern brush calligraphy.

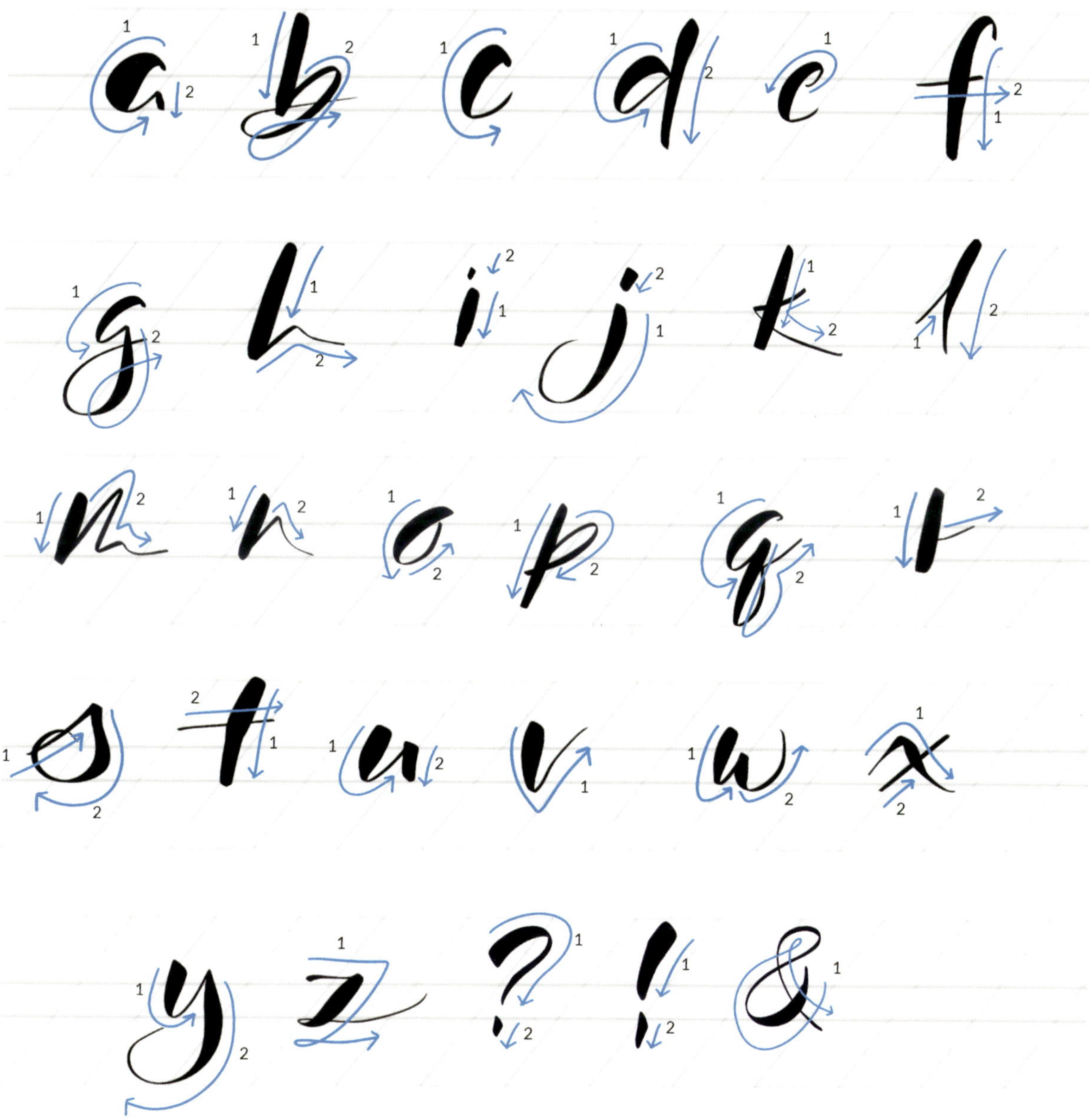

***Figure 33: Modern Brush Script lowercase letters***

### Uppercase letters

The uppercase letters in Modern Brush Script are written in a more straightforward manner in comparison to the three previous styles in the book. In order to maintain a similar aesthetic to the simpler form of the lowercase letters in this style, the capital letters here have fewer swirls and flourishes.

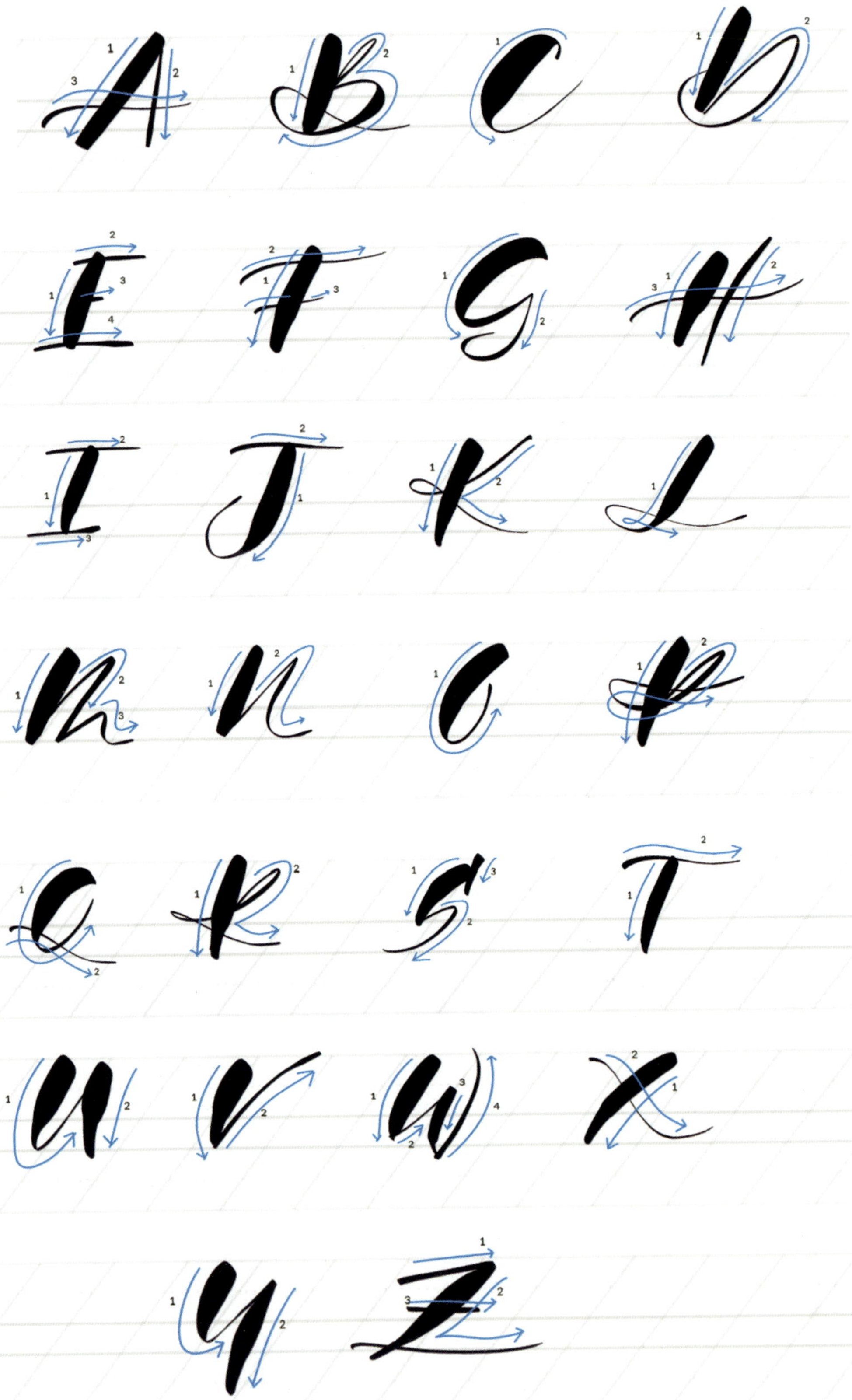

***Figure 34: Modern Brush Script uppercase letters***

**Forming words**

In Modern Brush Script, instead of having exit strokes that curve upwards like in the Basic Calligraphy style, it is preferable for the exit strokes to extend somewhat horizontally to connect to the next letter.

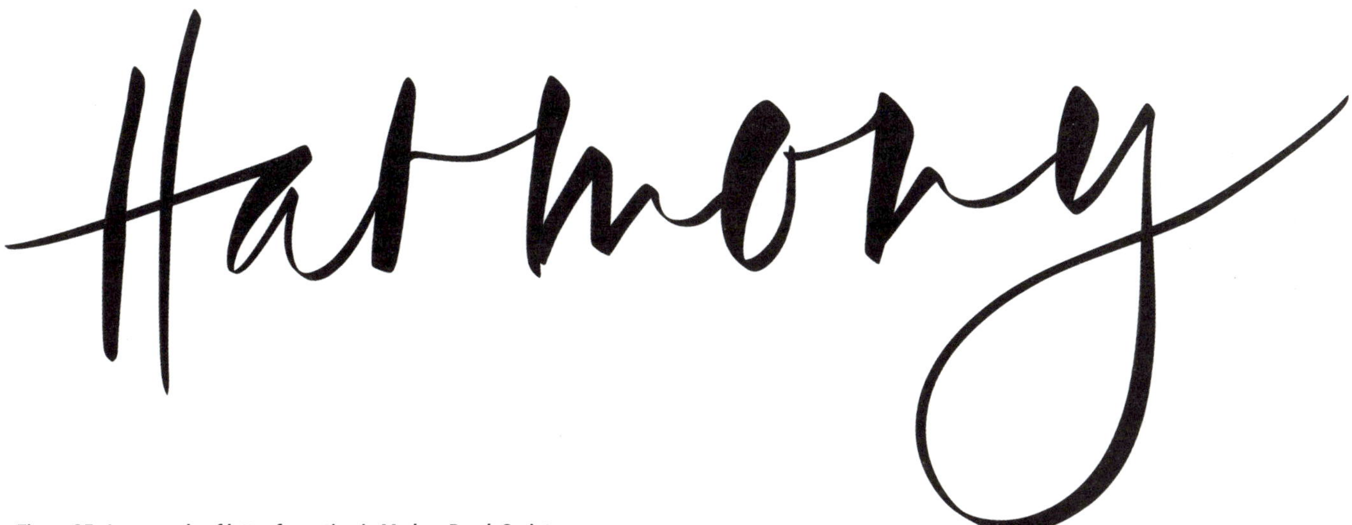


*Figure 35: An example of letter formation in Modern Brush Script*

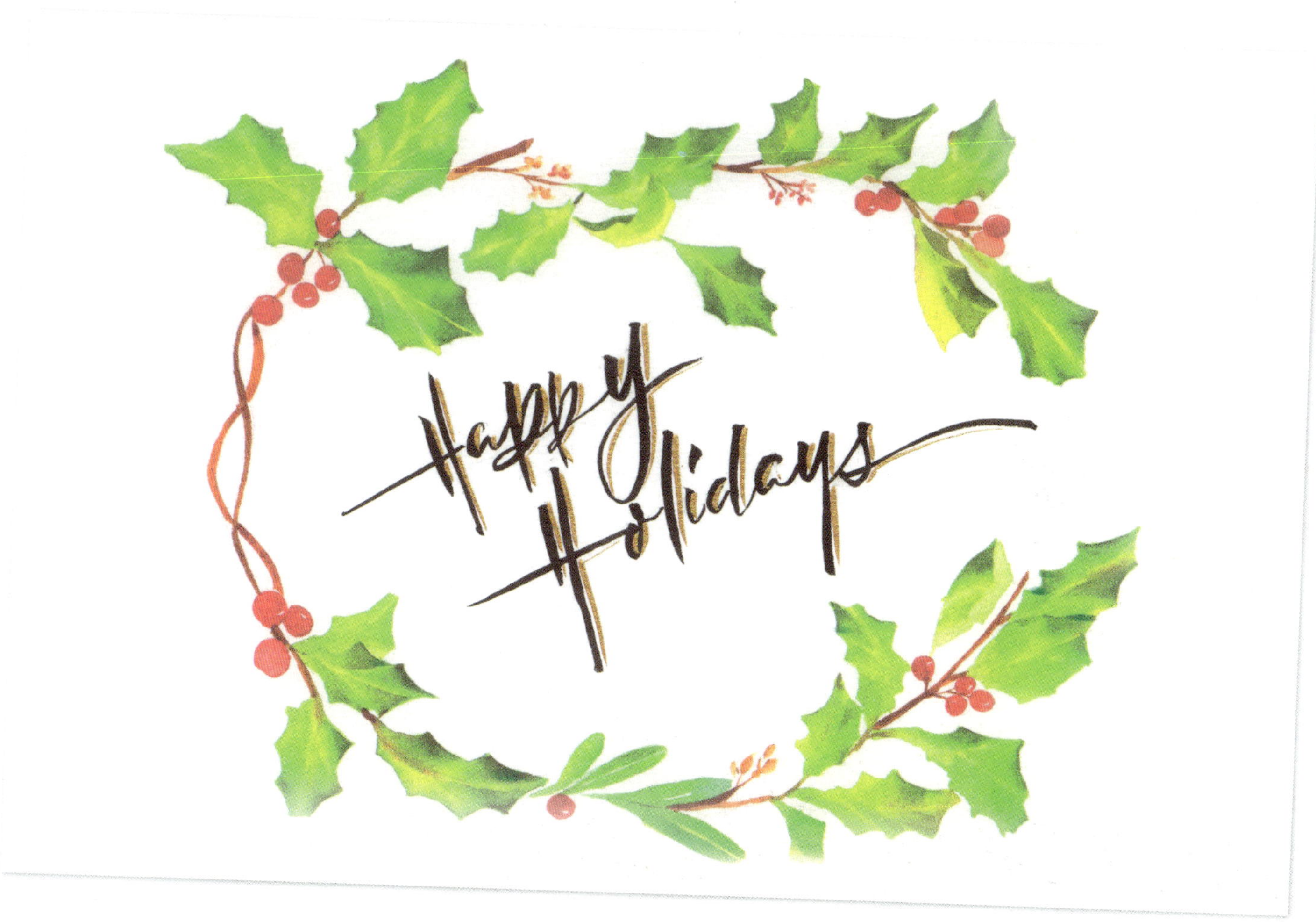

## FLOURISHED SCRIPT

Now, here comes the fun part! In previous sections, you've built up a foundation of basic strokes, learned the building blocks of Basic Calligraphy and explored how to vary the look of your final lettering style by making simple variations to the basic rules. In this section, you'll learn how to add decorative elements, otherwise known as flourishes, to your lettering. Although these flourishes don't contribute directly to legibility, they are an excellent way to add a creative flair to your words.

Many calligraphers and letterers add flourishes to their final work, and this isn't limited to only one particular application. It is very common to add some flourishes to final artwork or to make quotes look decorative. This style is great for adding accents to headings or when used for name and place cards, amongst others.

### Lowercase letters

We rarely flourish lowercase letters unless these letters happen to be the last letter of a word or phrase, in which case we usually only flourish the exit stroke. This is mainly due to legibility issues as well as making sure to use flourishing as an accent point rather than to congest your entire paragraph or quote with too many decorative elements.

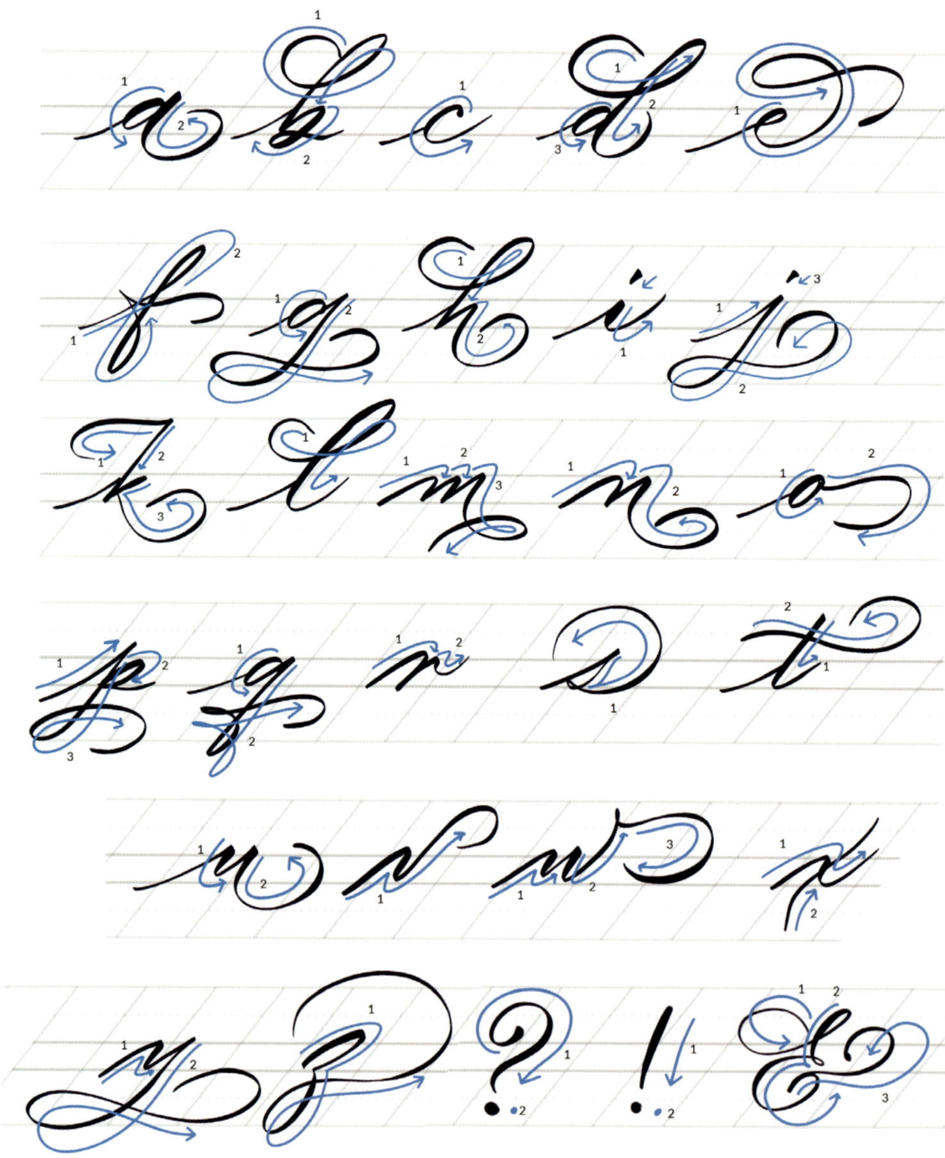

*Figure 36: Flourishing lowercase letters*

### Uppercase letters

As opposed to the lowercase letters, it is often a lot more fun to flourish uppercase letters as there is usually more room to play and explore with flourishing.

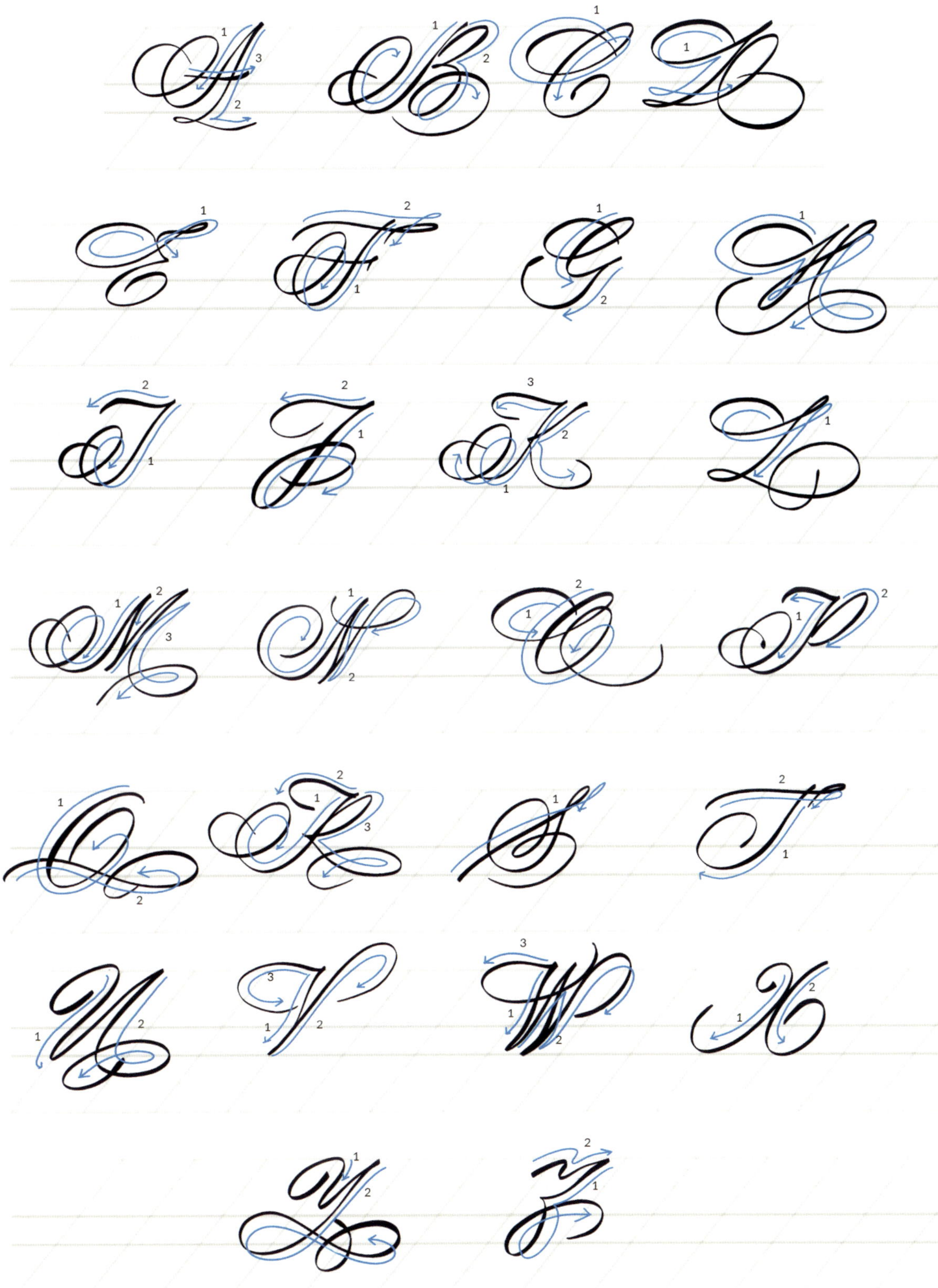

*Figure 37: Flourished Script uppercase letters*

### Flourishing words

The real test of your flourishing skills comes when you attempt to flourish words or layouts in a composition. In most cases, we start flourishing by focusing on the ascenders, the descenders, the capital stems, as well as the final, or exit, strokes of a letter. When flourishing a word, always aim to seek for balance in your final result. A balanced word is a word that isn't too heavy with flourishes on either the top, bottom, left or right of the word.

When you're just starting out, it may be challenging to try to figure out where and how to flourish these elements. As such, it's recommended that you add in flourishes as the last step, since it is only then that you can see the text as a whole and identify which parts require that extra bit of decoration.

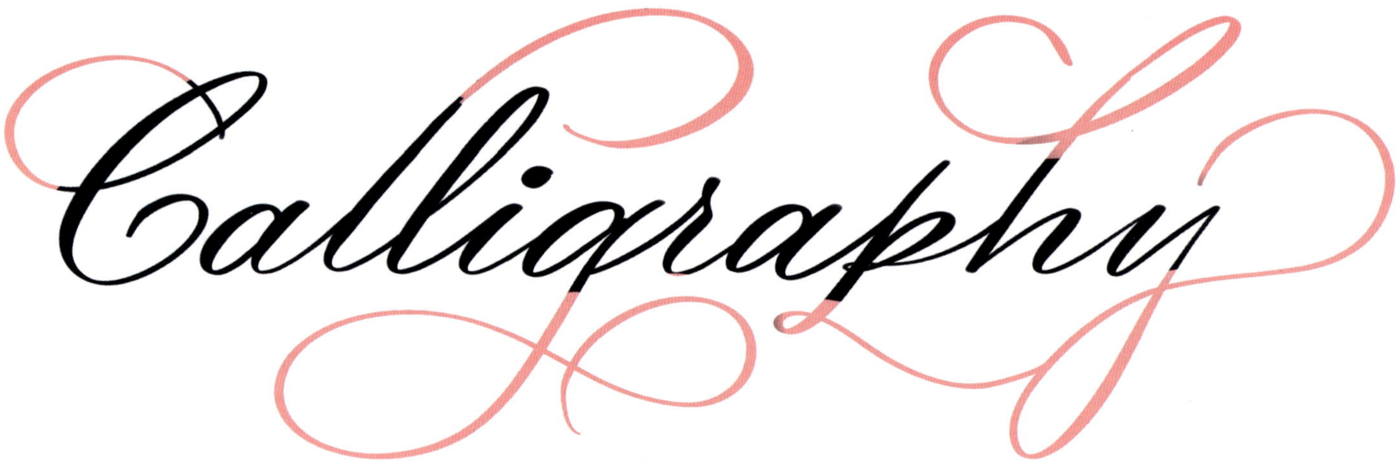


***Figure 38:** This flourished example illustrates which components of the letters can be flourished*

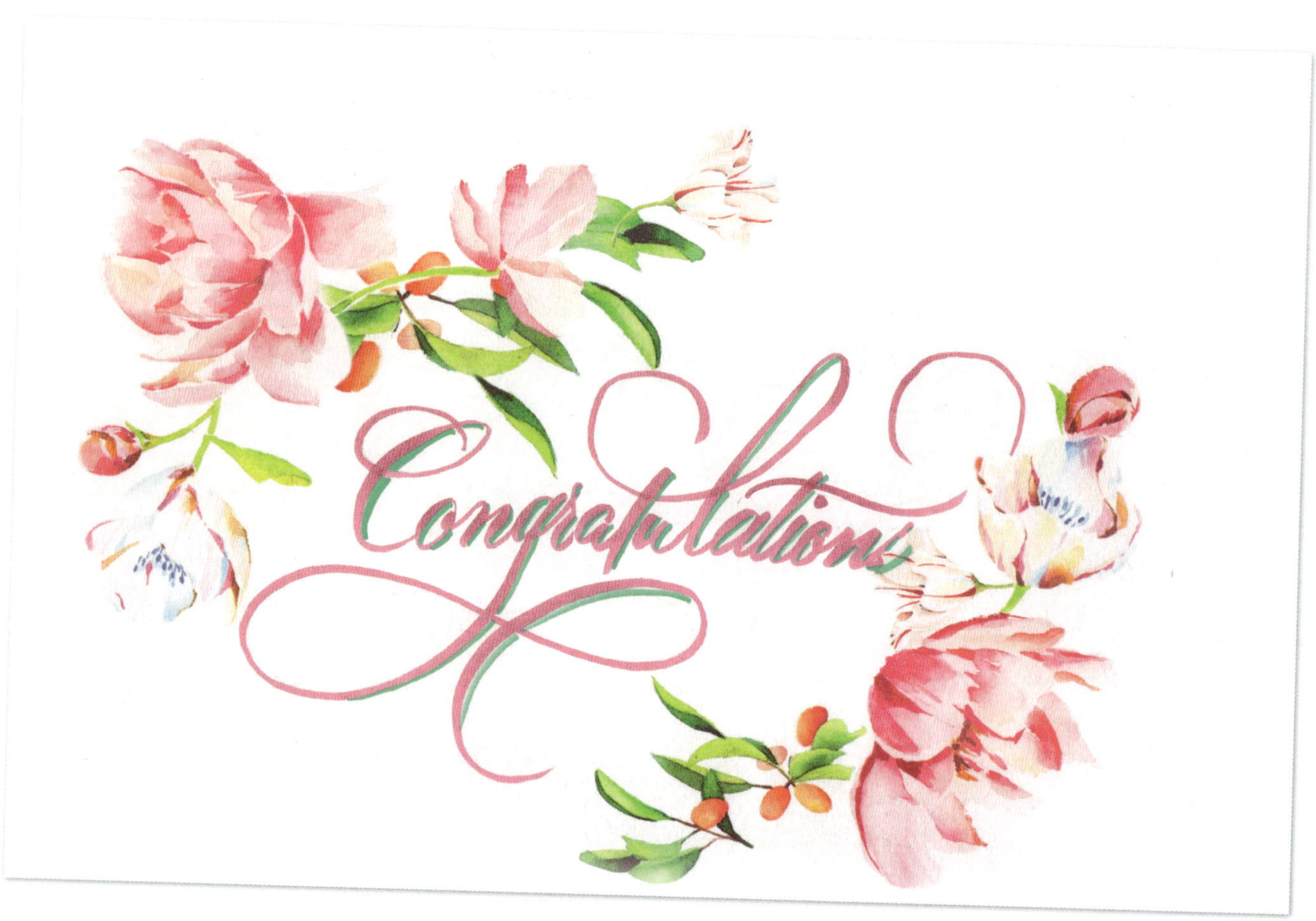

## UNCIAL

This version of Uncial is actually a modernised version of Half-Uncials, which was originally a style that fell halfway between Uncials written all in capitals and an alphabet composed of capitals and small letters. It has retained many features of the scripts used in the Book of Kells, the Lindisfarne Gospels and other books written in about the 8th century. At that time, capitals used for headings and to start paragraphs were often entirely different or extremely ornate so new capitals have been designed to go with these small letters.

When ruling your own guidelines on paper, the usual x-height of these Uncial letters is 41/2 nib-widths. Though some letters like 'b' and 'l' can be sloped, it is generally a vertical alphabet and the pen is maintained at a constant angle of your choice between 0° and 10°. The shape of all letters is controlled by the shape of the 'o'. The centre of the pen nib follows a circle, so the inside shape is narrower than a perfect circle and the outside is wider. It's often easiest to think about where the centre of the nib is moving while you write, or watch the white space inside the counter of letters as you create it.

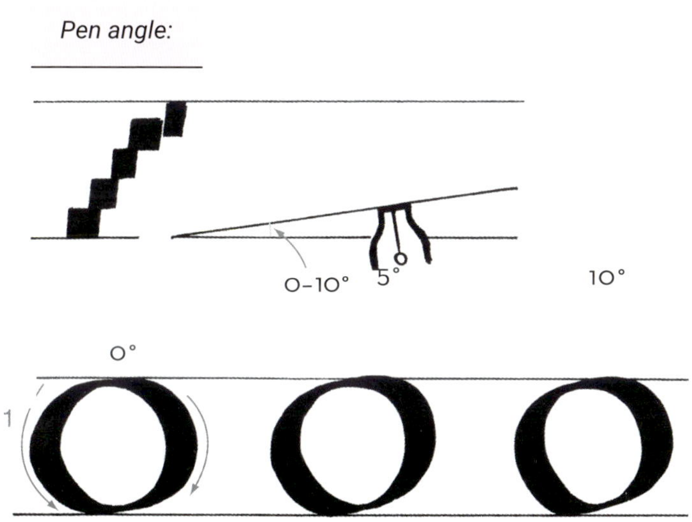


*Figure 39: The effect of different angle degrees on the letter 'o'*

One of the features of these letters is the big triangular serif.

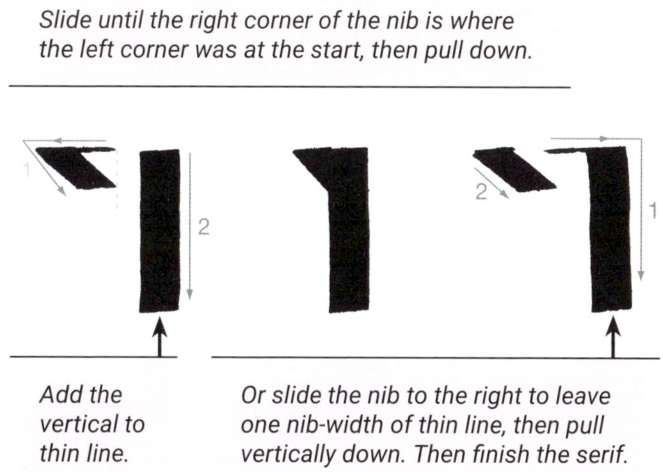


*Figure 40: Adding a triangular serif*

On some letters of the alphabet on the next page, like 'f', 'p', 'r' and 'q', the serif has been drawn below the top guideline and the curved part of each letter grows from it or on to it.

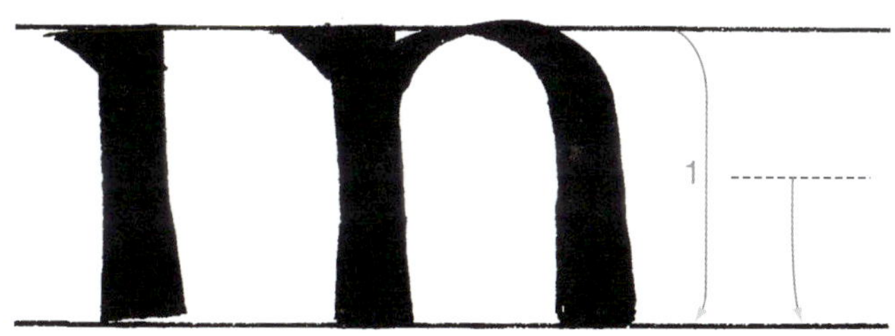


*Figure 41: Serif style drawn above and below the guidelines*

Originally, the lower end of a vertical stroke was wider than the top, due to the monks pressing harder on the quill and making the nib splay. If you would like to add this feature to letters, you can pull the nib a little to the left when you get close to the line, then add another stroke on the right.

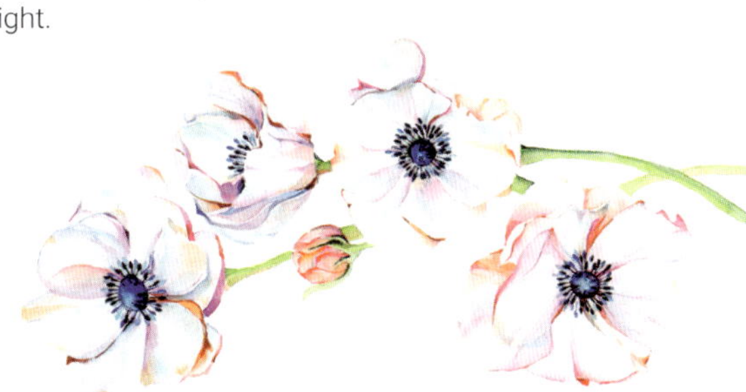

**Uncial lowercase letters and numbers**

Here is the lowercase alphabet and numbers for this style. You can practise them on page 44.

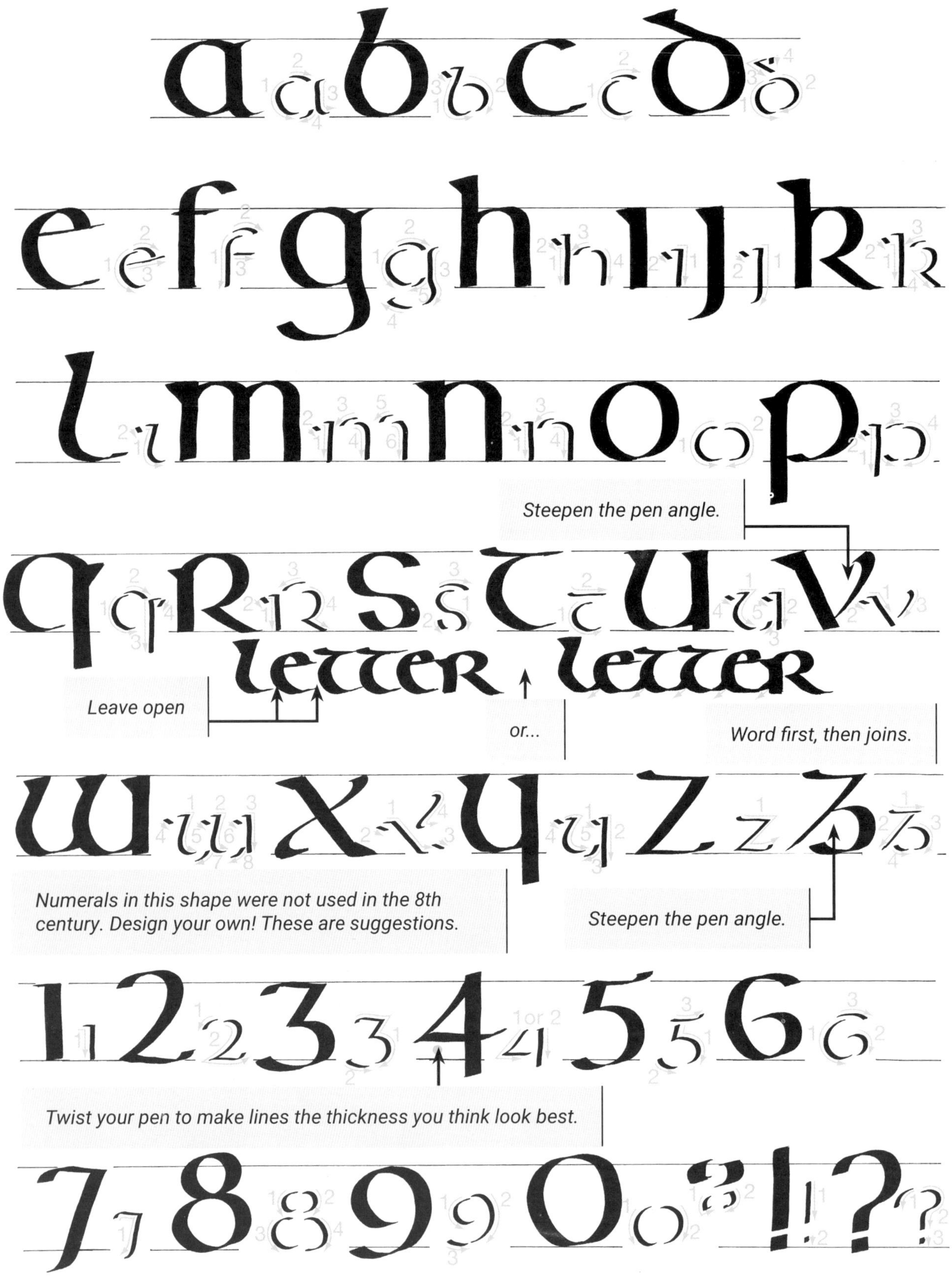


*Figure 42: Uncial lowercase letters and numbers*

### Uncial uppercase letters

Many of these modernised capitals are large versions of the small letters. The serifs on 'T' and 'Z' were partially drawn by pulling the wet ink on the letter into shape with the corner of the nib. The same technique can be used to shape the serif on 'D', if necessary. But you can twist your nib to create them any way you like.

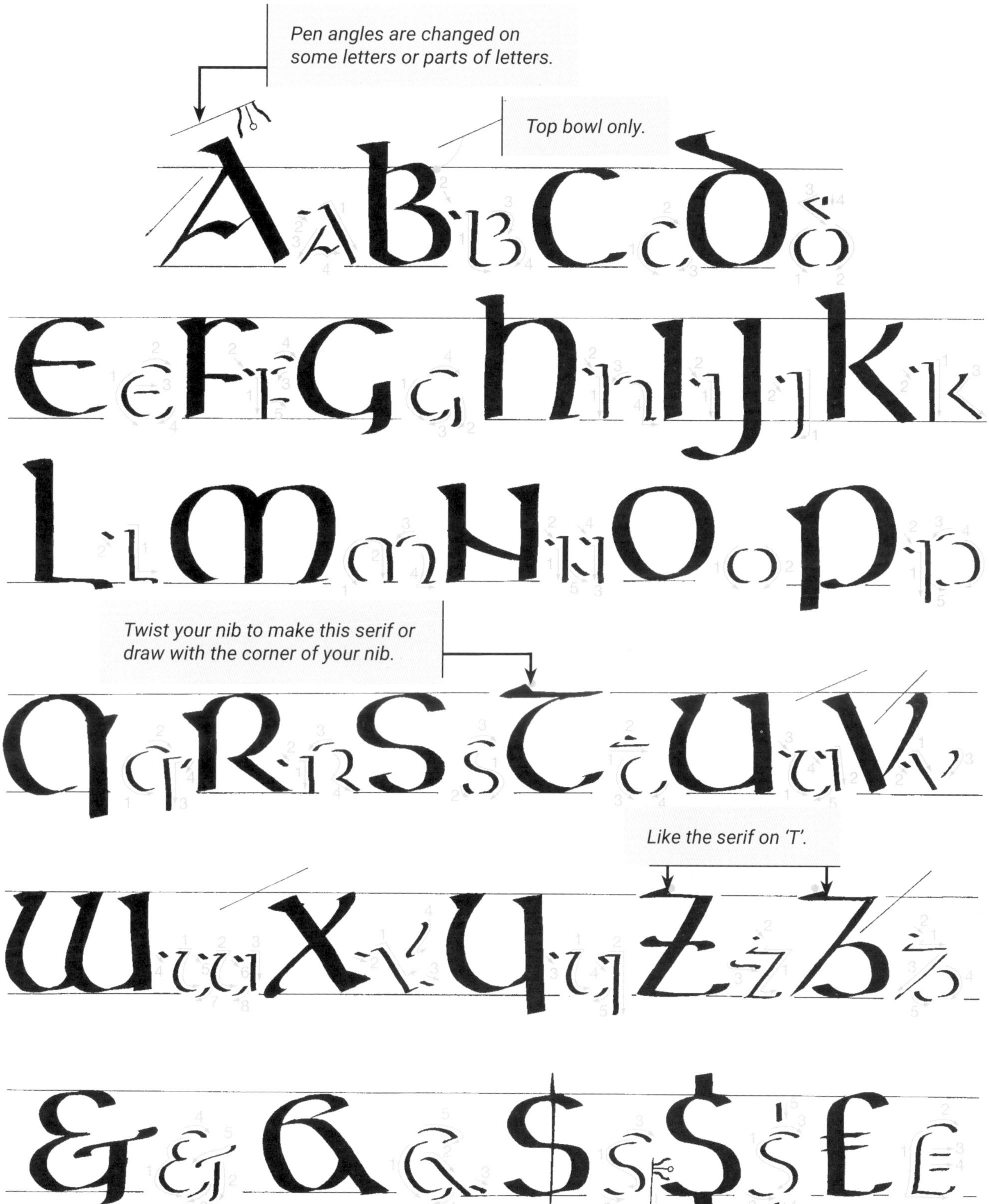


*Figure 43: Uncial uppercase letters*

# CREATING CALLIGRAPHIC ART

Now that you've learned all about the technical aspects of calligraphy, it's time to unleash your inner artist and use your newly acquired knowledge to create beautiful and lasting artefacts, express yourself and inspire others!

In the modern age of mass-production, calligraphy is a wonderful way to create personalised, handmade keepsakes to treasure for a lifetime. As an artform, it offers so may creative possibilities, ranging from greeting cards, to posters and prints that you can keep for yourself or give to loved ones as a beautiful handmade gift. It's time to take what you have learned about calligraphy and show your skills to the world!

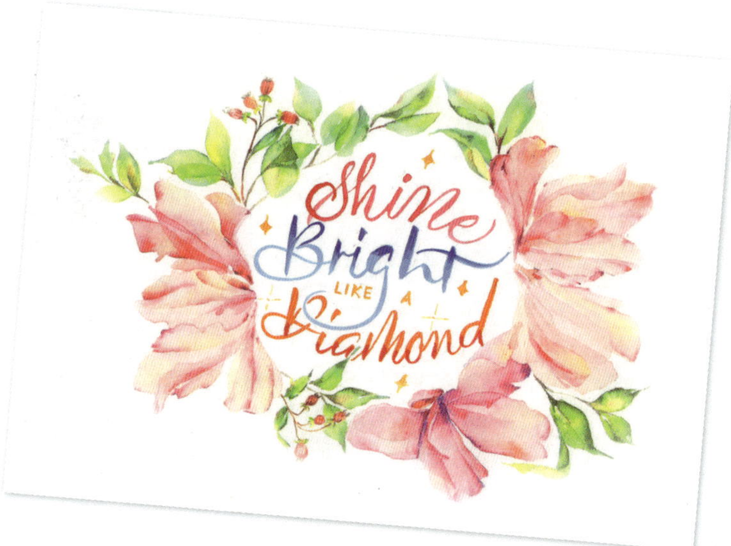


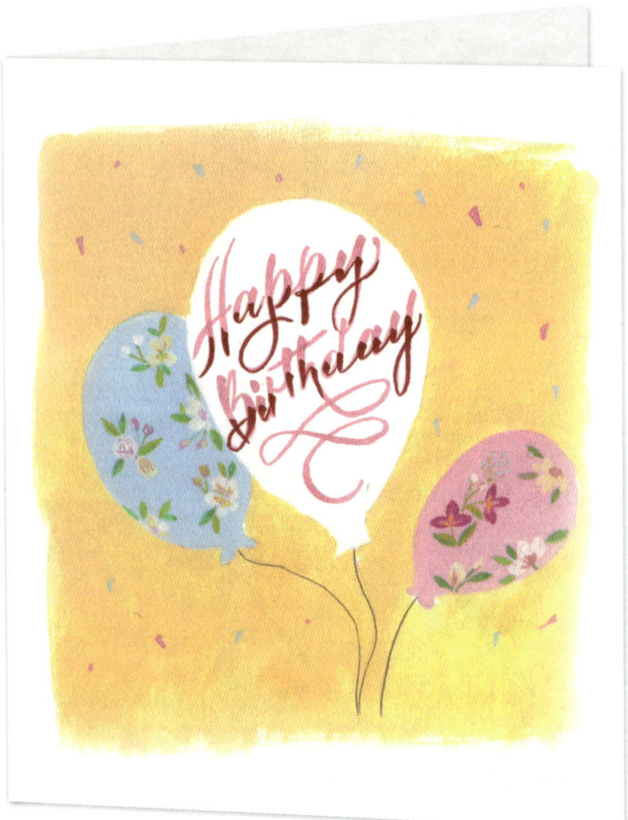


Make the written word even more powerful and permanent by creating beautiful handwritten letters, notes and greetings cards. Create unique gifts for friends and family, such as bookmarks, poems and affirmations cards. Add style and grace to a celebration by creating place cards, menus and signs. Inspire others with motivational posters and empowering prints adorned with your favourite quotes.

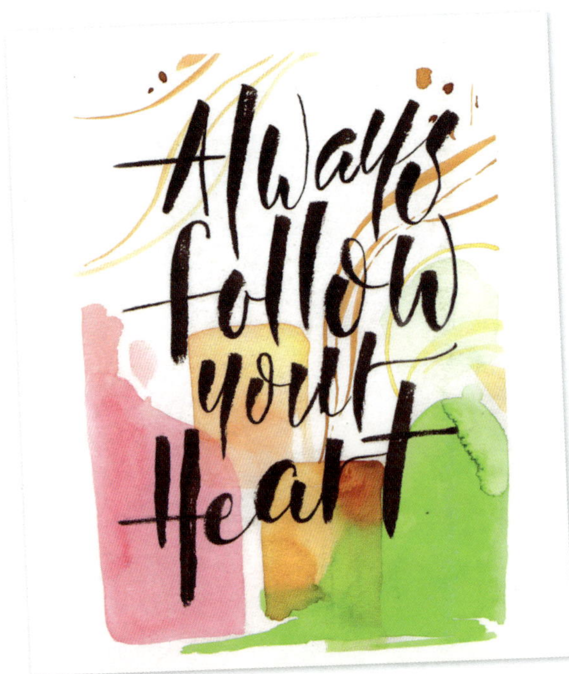


While technical skills are the foundation of beautiful calligraphy, what will make your creations special is expressing your own feelings, mood and personality. You've done all the hard work learning the basics, so now it's time to have some fun! Get out your calligraphy toolbox, grab some colourful markers and let your creativity run free!

# PRACTICE MAKES PERFECT



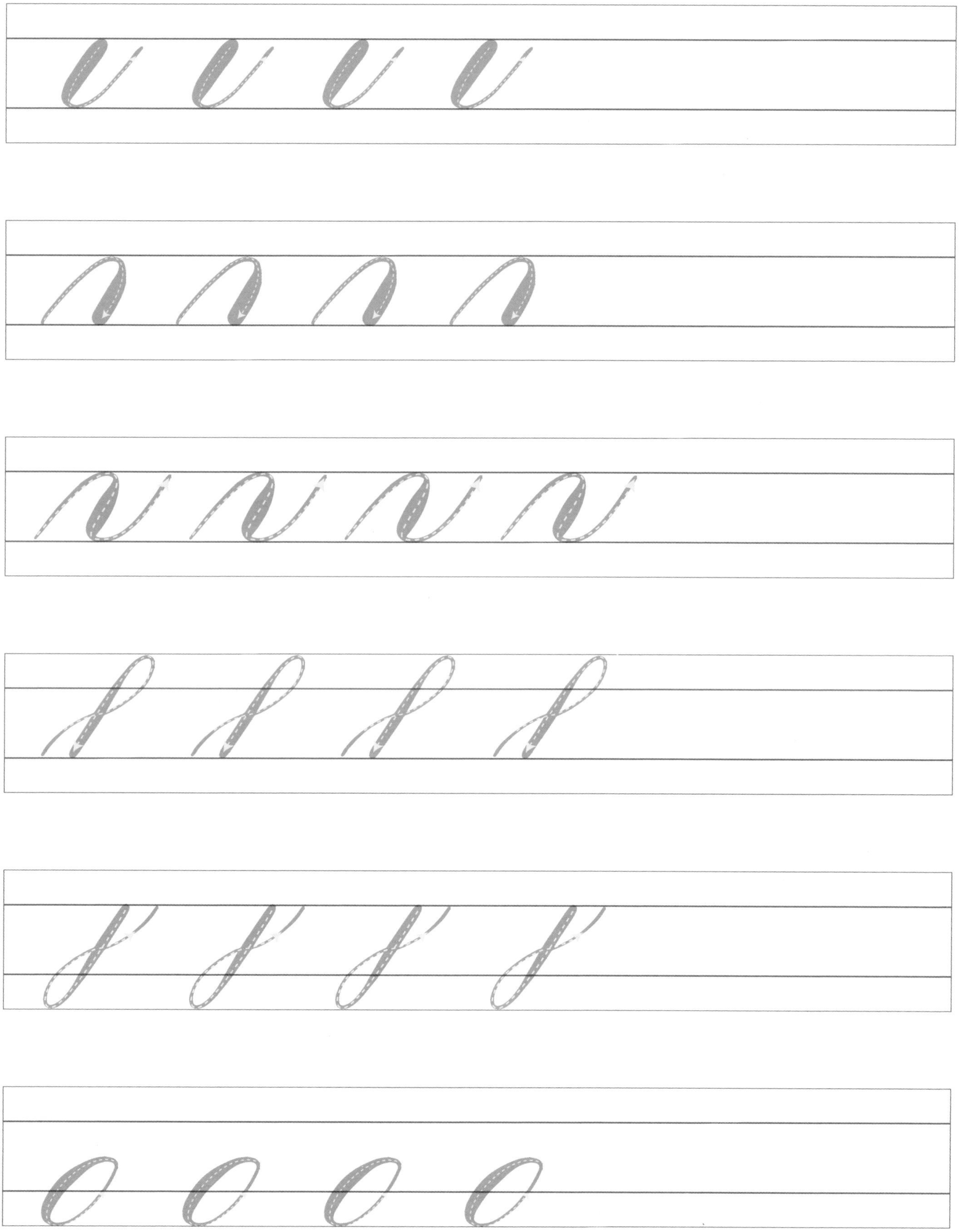

a b c d e f
g h i j k l
m n o p q r
s t u v w x
y z

A B C D E F

G H I J K L

M N O P Q R

S T U V W X

Y Z

a b c d e f g h

i j k l m n o p

q r s t u v w

x y z

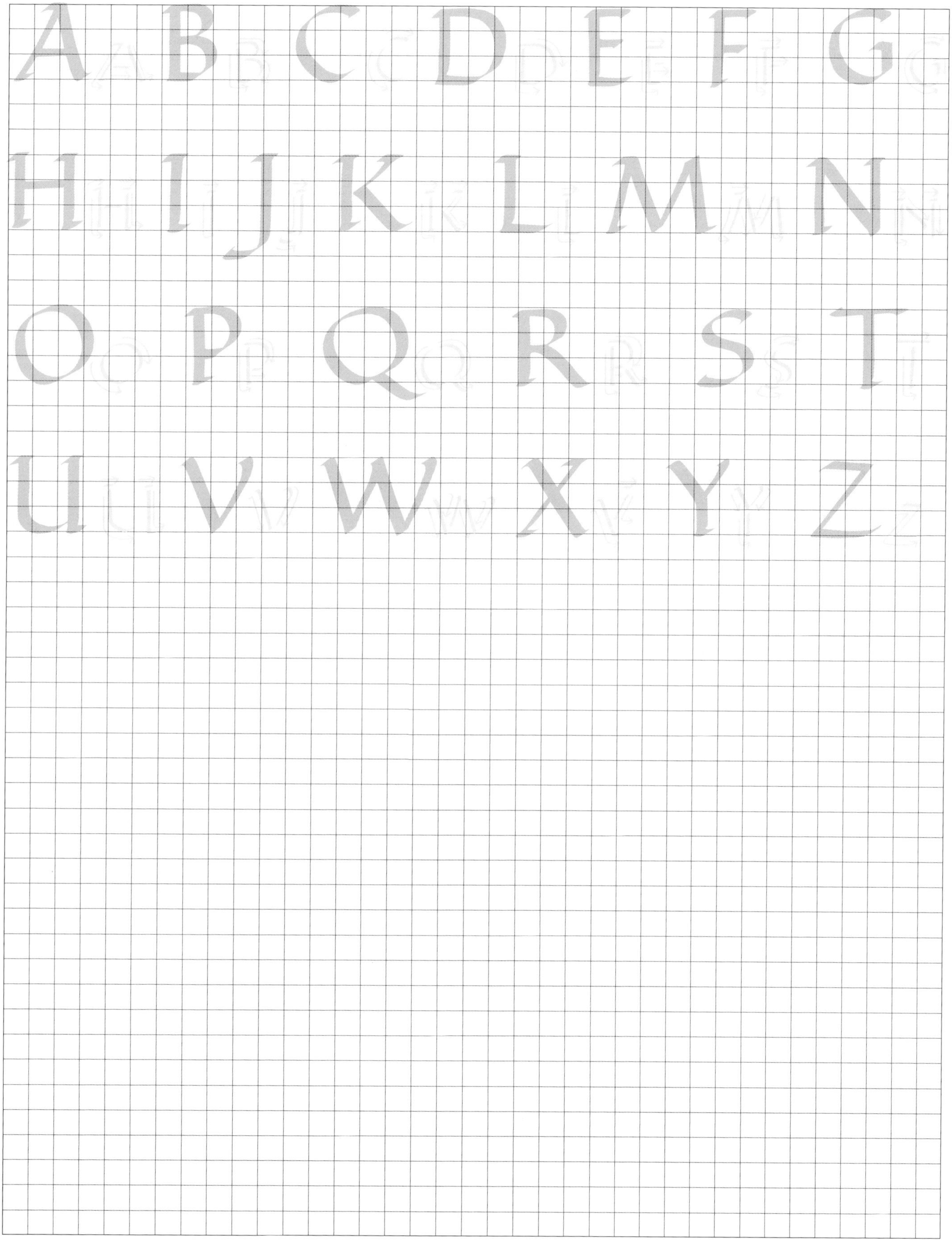
A B C D E F G
H I J K L M N
O P Q R S T
U V W X Y Z

a b c d e f g h i

j k l m n o p q

r s t u v w x y z

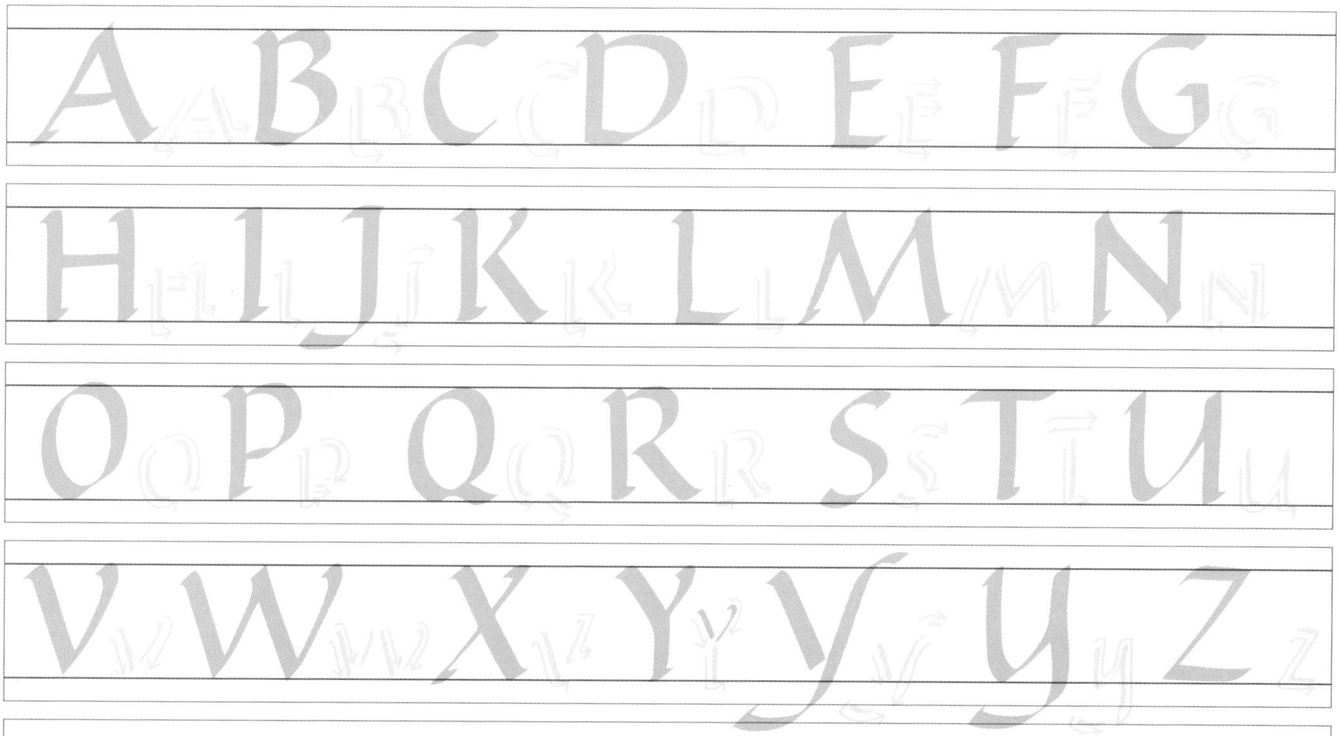

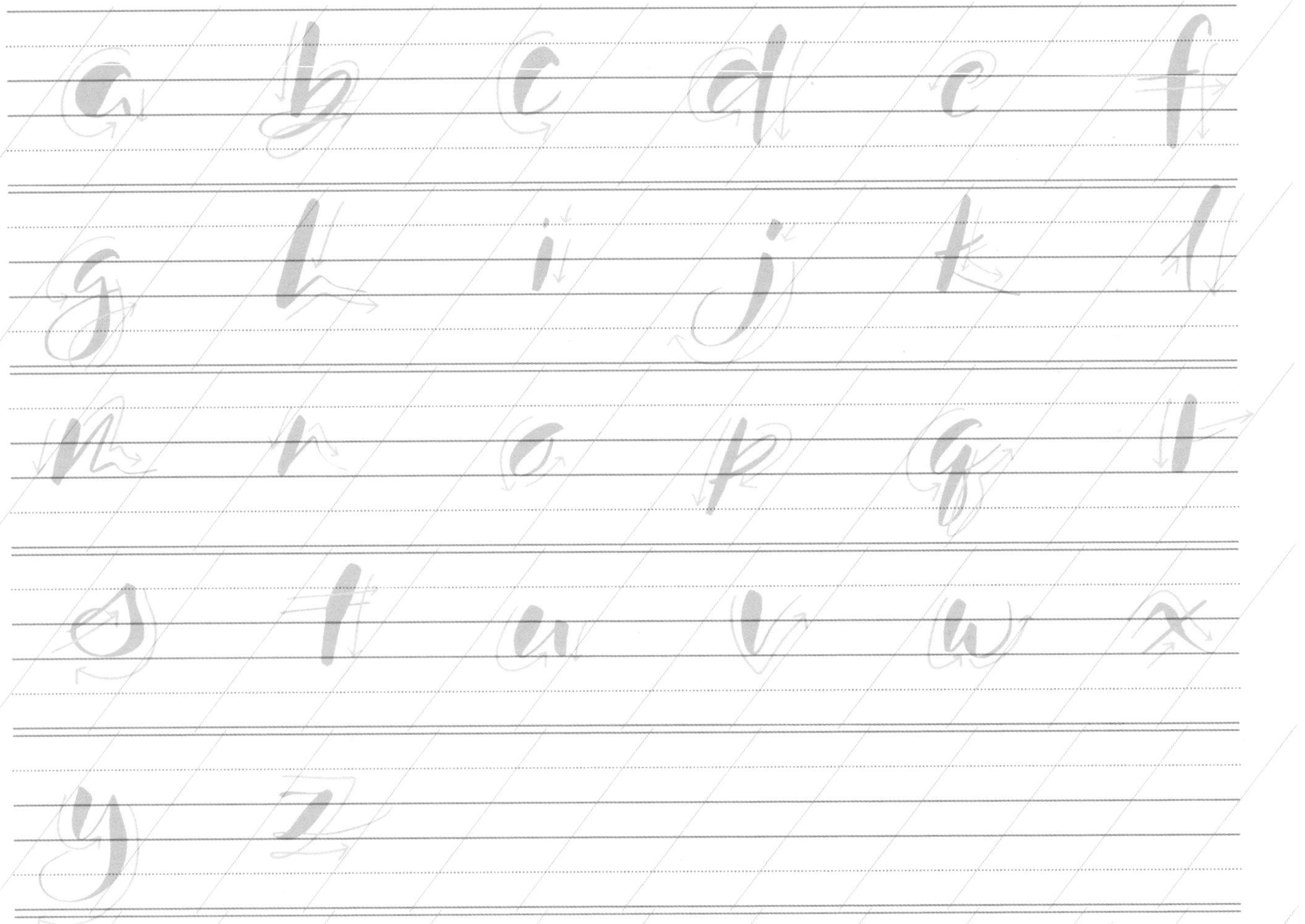

## Modern Brush Script/ Uppercase letters

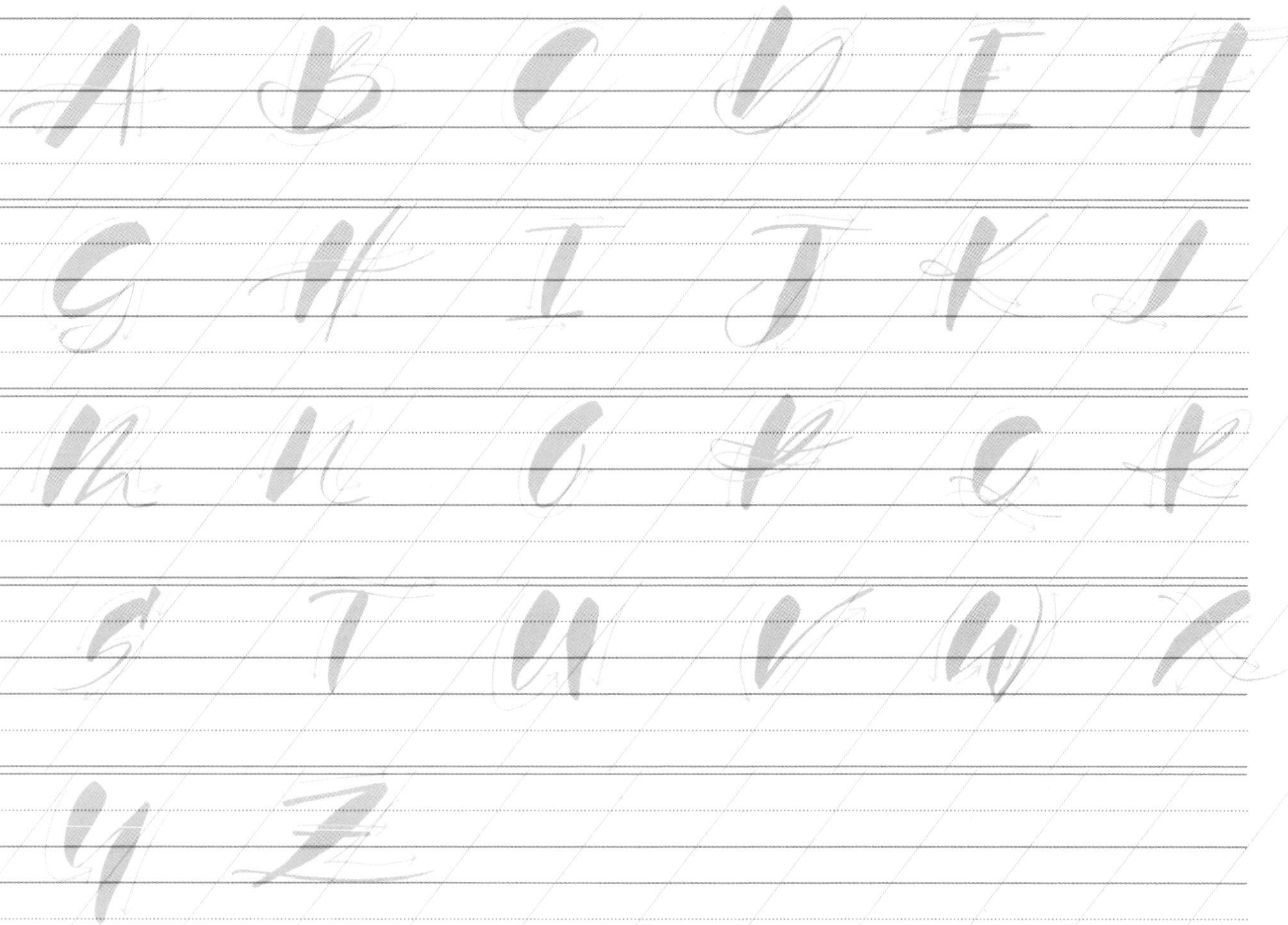

# Flourished Script/ Lowercase letters

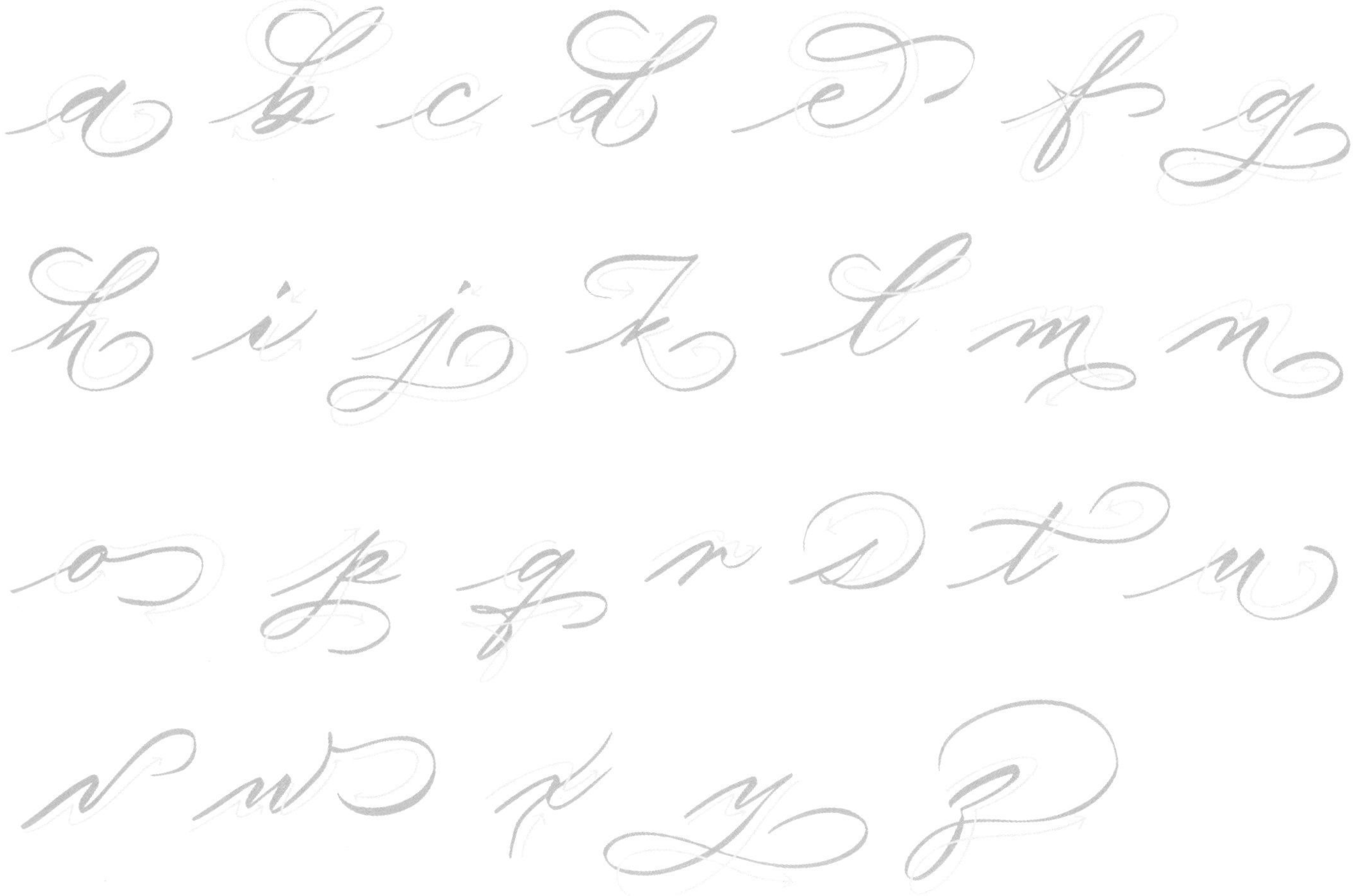

## Flourished Script/ Uppercase letters

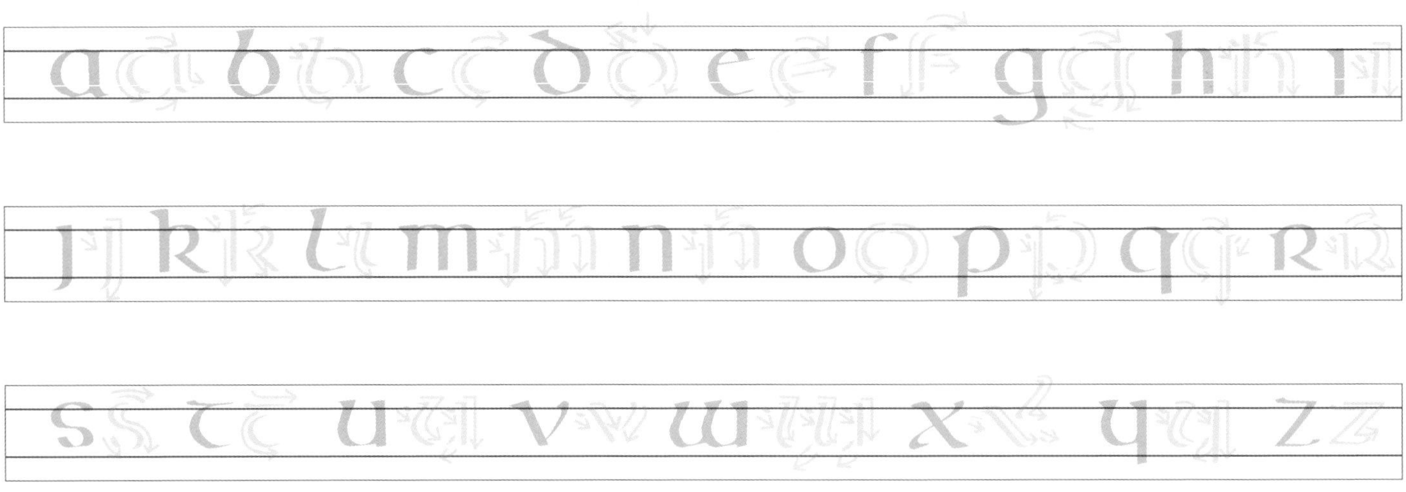

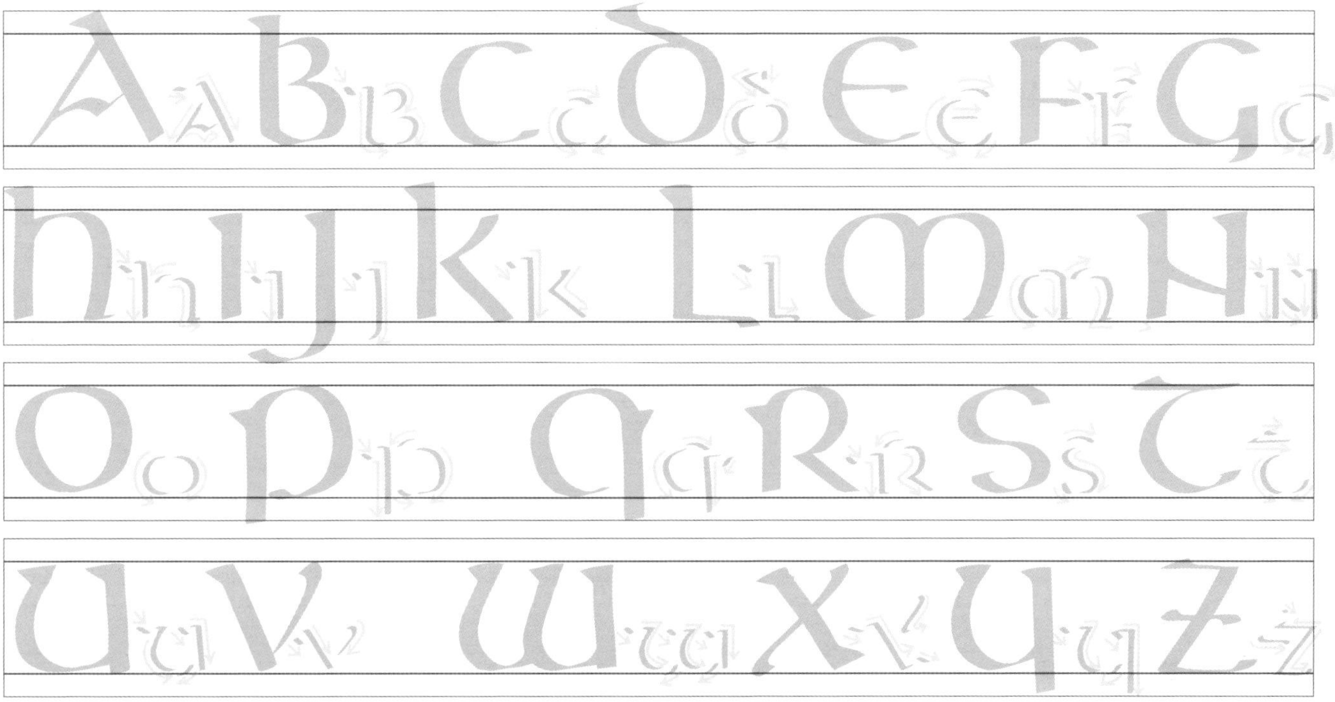

Basic Calligraphy Practice Page, brush marker

Basic Calligraphy Practice Page, brush marker

Foundational Hand Practice Page, nib width = 1.9 mm

Foundational Hand Practice Page, nib width = 1.9 mm

Foundational Hand Practice Page, nib width = 1.9 mm

Foundational Hand Practice Page, nib width = 1.9 mm

Foundational Hand Practice Page, nib width = 1.9 mm

Italic Practice Page, nib width = 1.1 mm

Italic Practice Page, nib width = 1.1 mm

Italic Practice Page, nib width = 1.1 mm

Italic Practice Page, nib width = 1.1 mm

Italic Practice Page, nib width = 1.1 mm

Modern Brush Script Practice Page, brush marker

Modern Brush Script Practice Page, brush marker

Flourished Script Practice page, any nib width

Flourished Script Practice page, any nib width

Flourished Script Practice page, any nib width

Uncial Practice Page, nib width = 1.1 mm

Uncial Practice Page, nib width = 1.1 mm

Uncial Practice Page, nib width = 1.1 mm

Uncial Practice Page, nib width = 1.1 mm

Uncial Practice Page, nib width = 1.1 mm